IS YOUR NEIGHBOR
A ZOMBIE?

In loving memory of
Pablo Wallerstein Manonellas, 1986–2001
El mundo es más pobre sin ti

First published in the USA and Great Britain in 2014

Conceived and produced by
Elwin Street Productions
3 Percy Street
London, W1T 1DE
United Kingdom
www.elwinstreet.com

Bloomsbury USA, 1385 Broadway, New York, NY 10018
Bloomsbury Publishing Plc, 50 Bedford Square, London WC1B 3DP

www.bloomsbury.com

Bloomsbury is a trademark of Bloomsbury Publishing Plc

Bloomsbury Publishing, New York, London, New Delhi, Sydney

Library of Congress Cataloging-In-Publication data has been applied for
A CIP catalogue record for this book is available from the British Library

US ISBN: 978-1-62040-841-4
UK ISBN: 978-1-40885-813-4

10 9 8 7 6 5 4 3 2 1

Printed and bound in China

IS YOUR NEIGHBOR
A ZOMBIE?

COMPELLING PHILOSOPHICAL PUZZLES
THAT CHALLENGE YOUR BELIEFS

JEREMY STANGROOM

BLOOMSBURY
NEW YORK · LONDON · NEW DELHI · SYDNEY

CONTENTS

INTRODUCTION 6

I
RED BALL OR BLACK BALL? 8
Classic logical conundrums and paradoxes

· Red Ball or Black Ball? 10
· Is the Elevator Malfunctioning? 12
· What Colour is Your Raven? 14
· Is Small and Happy Best? 16
· Why Did the Barber Flee Town? 18
· Valid or Invalid? 20
· What Will the Crocodile Do? 22
· What's Going on with the Androids? 24

2
IS YOUR NEIGHBOR A ZOMBIE? 26
Problems exploring the mind and perceptions of personal identity

· Is Your Neighbor a Zombie? 28
· Can You Be Responsible for What is Unavoidable? 30
· Is Tom Pearce Tom Pearce? 32
· What's My Potential? 34
· Who Gets Tortured? 36

3
WHAT IF MONTY DOESN'T KNOW? 38
Classic puzzles and thought experiments revisited

· What if Monty Doesn't Know? 40
· Should You Run Over the Fat Man? 42
· Is Zeus Losing His Power? 44
· Is it Necessarily Wrong to Eat People? 46

4
HOW OBEDIENT ARE WE? 48
Puzzles that affect society and group behaviour

· What's Going to Happen at the Robbers' Cave? 50
· Is Homo Sapiens a Noble Savage? 52
· Will Help Arrive? 54
· Whom Do You Prefer? 56
· How about a Date? 58
· How Obedient are We? 60
· Who Should Lizzy Choose? 62

5
WHEN IS A BELIEF NOT A BELIEF? 64
Thought experiments challenging the concepts of belief and reality

· Is it Rational to Believe in Monsters Under the Bed? 66
· When is a Belief Not a Belief? 68
· Are We Brains in Vats? 70
· Did We Evolve to Know About the World? 72

Solutions 74
Index 142

INTRODUCTION

If you write a book that aims to show that people often think badly, then you run the risk of falling into hubris. So perhaps it's appropriate to start with a confession. If I had come across the puzzles featured here without the benefit of foreknowledge, then I would have gone wrong, often and disastrously.

However, my shortcomings in this regard are shared by many people. Lots of us don't think particularly well, and the merit of a book such as this one is that it encourages a certain humility with respect to our own abilities. Consider, for example, the following scenario.

You're the leader of a country that is facing the outbreak of an epidemic that will kill exactly 600 people if you don't do something about it. Your top medical advisors have prepared two alternative programs to combat the disease and have estimated the likely consequences of adopting each program. You can be confident that these estimates are accurate.

Program A — 200 people will be saved.

Program B — there is a one-third probability that 600 people will be saved and a two-thirds probability that no people will be saved.

Which program do you prefer?

Okay, now imagine it's a few years later, and you're facing precisely the same situation. An epidemic that's going to kill exactly 600 people is on its way, and again you have two medical programs available to you.

Program A — 400 people will die.

Program B — there is a one-third probability that nobody will die and a two-thirds probability that 600 people will die.

Which program do you prefer this time around?

There is no correct answer to these questions, but did you spot the trick? The choices available to you in both scenarios are identical. Program A means that 200 people will be saved and 400 will die; and Program B means there's a one-third probability that nobody will die and a two-thirds probability that 600 people will die.

If you chose Program A first time around and Program B second time, then although you likely made a cognitive error (unless, of course, you recognised the options were the same, but changed your mind), you responded as most people respond to these scenarios. The research of psychologists Daniel Kahneman and Amos Tversky indicates that more than 70 per cent of people will favour Program A if the choice is framed in the manner of Decision 1. However, if it is framed in the manner of Decision 2, then more than 75 per cent will favour Program B.

There is actually something a little startling about how easily we are led astray here. We tend to pride ourselves on our cognitive abilities, yet in this case most people's judgements are driven by contextual clues of which they're not even aware.

The puzzles, paradoxes and conundrums in this book provide plenty of similar opportunities for you to make cognitive errors. If you find yourself getting in a muddle, then rest assured you're not alone, and hopefully, even if it turns out there's little chance you'll be competing with Mr Spock for first prize in the Logic Olympics, you'll have some fun along the way.

1

RED BALL OR GREEN BALL?

Logic is like the sword – those who appeal to it, shall perish by it.
SAMUEL BUTLER

The puzzles featured in this chapter include logic problems, probability conundrums and fiendish paradoxes. A number of them are straightforward in the sense that they have right and wrong answers that can be calculated, albeit the logic involved is often a little tricky. However, there are also several conundrums here that do not have generally agreed solutions. In these cases, if you can see a way through the murk, then you're doing better than the professionals who make a career out of worrying about these sorts of things.

It is worth pointing out that there is nothing 'tricksy' about the puzzles in this chapter, or indeed, in future chapters. So, for example, there is no misleading wording here to throw you off track. The puzzles are real, not merely a function of the way that they are presented.

RED BALL OR GREEN BALL?

Frank Savage, owner of Chudleigh-by-the-Pond's premier snooker club, Balls 'R' Us, is having a bad day. His cunning plan to swipe the World Snooker Championship from sunny Sheffield has hit a bump in the baize as a result of some shenanigans involving a colourblind snooker player and a red, or possibly green, ball.

The trouble started during a game between Jim and Jules, the fiercest of local rivals, after Jim accused Jules of potting a green ball rather than the required red. Jules did not take kindly to this accusation, opining that Jim's colourblindness somewhat undermined his credibility as a witness. A row ensued, cues were raised, curses thrown and the rumpus only came to an end when Jim stomped off taking with him a clutch of red balls.

Unfortunately, this turn of events has left Frank short of the requisite number of red balls for tonight's Greater Chudleigh Cue for the Ages snooker tournament. There is some hope in the guise of Dennis Davis, owner of Chudleigh-by-the Pond's other, less salubrious, snooker venue, The Pocket Palace, but he's playing hardball. He tells Frank that he'll only let him have the balls he needs if he is able to win them in a game of chance.

There are two urns containing red and green balls, from which a ball will be drawn at random. This is how the balls will be distributed:

	URN A	URN B
No. of balls	100	100
Ratio of red to green balls	Uknown, all combinations equally likely	50:50

As you can see, Urn A could contain no red balls or 100 red balls, since all combinations of red and green balls are equally likely. Urn B is known to contain 50 red balls and 50 green balls).

Davis explains to Frank that he must choose which urn he wants to draw the ball from. If the red ball is drawn, then Frank gets to keep it and another draw will be made (after the urn is replenished with a new red ball). If the green ball is drawn, then the game is over, and it's time for Frank to go home.

Assuming that Frank wants to maximise the chances of a red ball being drawn, which urn should he pick for his first choice?

SOLUTION ON PAGE 76

IS THE ELEVATOR MALFUNCTIONING?

The villagers of Chudleigh-by-the-Pond are rightly proud of the village's newest skyscraper, Billy Brewer Tower. Built to zero-energy specifications, and incorporating the latest in building-integrated photovoltaic technology, it is an architectural and engineering marvel. It's a shame then, that its single elevator appears to be malfunctioning.

The problem has come to light as a result of a disagreement between Peter and Eloise, both residents of the building. Peter has been hired as a private tutor by Eloise's uncle to help her prepare for her Finals at Bovey Institute of Technology. Unfortunately, he has a habit of turning up late for their lessons despite the fact that he only has to get himself from his apartment to her apartment.

Eloise confronted him about his tardiness and he explained that he is having difficulty with the elevator. It always seems to be going in the wrong direction. To get to her apartment, he needs to head upwards, but the elevator apparently has a preference for going downwards, which means he has to wait until it returns from the ground floor before he is able to catch it.

This struck Eloise as a pretty poor excuse; he should just leave a bit earlier. However, her interest was piqued because she too had experienced a problem with the elevator, only in the opposite direction. In her experience, whenever she summons the elevator, it tends to arrive while travelling upwards, which means she has to wait until it completes its upwards journey before catching it down to street level.

Obviously, they can't both be right, so they decide to test their observations in a more rigorous manner. However, they are rather startled to find that their perceptions are accurate. If you catch the elevator from Peter's floor, then it's much more likely to arrive on a downwards rather than upwards journey. But if you catch it from Eloise's floor, it's the other way around — it tends to arrive on its way up to the top floor.

So what's going on here? Is the elevator malfunctioning or is there some other explanation for its strange behaviour?

SOLUTION ON PAGE 79

WHAT COLOUR IS YOUR RAVEN?

A dispute has broken out between amateur ornithologists, Davina Corvus and Bill Taube, about the identity of a rather homely looking bird they have spotted. Corvus insists that the bird's fine beak identifies it as an urban raven, native to the Trafalgaris region. Taube, for his part, thinks it's a pigeon, mainly because it looks like a pigeon, but also because all ravens are black, and this bird is not black.

Taube points this out, but is rather taken aback when Corvus simply denies that all ravens are black, claiming that some ravens have evolved pigeon-like characteristics in a bid to avoid servitude at the Tower of London. She insists that Taube provide at least some evidence to back up a claim that on the face of it seems rather exclusionary.

Happily, Taube once took an Access course in philosophy, so knows that he can easily provide evidence to support his claim. He reaches into his pocket, pulls out a red apple, and waves it under Corvus's nose. Corvus is unimpressed and scoffs at the notion that the mere existence of a red apple supports the claim that all ravens are black.

Can the existence of a red apple support the claim that all ravens are black?

SOLUTION ON PAGE 81

CHAPTER 1

QUICKIE 1

A murderer is condemned to death. He has to choose between three rooms. The first is full of raging fires, the second is full of assassins with loaded guns, and the third is full of lions that haven't eaten in three years.

Which room is safest for him?

(SOLUTIONS ON PAGE 140)

QUICKIE 2

Two mothers and two daughters go shopping. They have $21, which they split equally between them.

How can this be possible?

IS SMALL AND HAPPY BEST?

It's the year 2184 and the Earth has been conquered by aliens. The invaders claim that they're from Mars and say that they mean no harm to the uncivilized, bloodthirsty, barbarians — i.e. us — who have up until this point had the Earth all to themselves. And so far, it's got to be said, apart from a rather messy culinary misunderstanding involving a royal corgi, they have been gracious and generous in victory.

However, things have recently taken a rather troubling turn. It seems the Martians are concerned that Planet Earth has one too many countries and they've convened an official commission to determine which country should be 'phased out'. Happily, assurances have been given that there will be no compulsory deaths.

This process is now almost at an end and the field has been narrowed to two countries. A representative from each country is about to give a presentation explaining why their country should be spared. The only criterion in play at this final stage is a quality of life index.

Ronald Plump, the delegate from the Isle of Gold, is confident that he's going to win the day. The Isle of Gold has a small, hugely affluent population and there is plenty of research that demonstrates that everybody living there is perfectly content. Sovetia, on the other hand, has a vast population, many times the size of the population of the Isle of Gold and it is generally agreed, even by the Sovetians themselves, that lives in Sovetia are barely worth living.

Plump is therefore a little surprised to see Lindsey Rees, the Sovetian delegate, wandering around looking confident, and perhaps even a little smug. Plump asks her what's going on and she explains that she's been attending classes led by ex-policeman and peripatetic philosopher, Inspector Morse, and that she has a surefire way of demonstrating that however bad things are in Sovetia, the situation is no worse than it is in the Isle of Gold.

Plump is incredulous, but Inspector Morse has a reputation for showing that the impossible is possible, so he's slightly nervous about what Rees has up her sleeve.

Is he right to be nervous? How is Lindsey Rees going to demonstrate that the situation in Sovetia is no worse than it is in the Isle of Gold?

SOLUTION ON PAGE 84

WHY DID THE BARBER FLEE TOWN?

Samson has recently been elected mayor of Zorah after narrowly winning a disputed election. A rumour has begun circulating around the town that he only managed to secure victory by slaughtering large swathes of the opposition's support with the jawbone of an ass. This might sound implausible, but as the townspeople are apt to point out, it's a lot more credible than the alternative theory that he got into power as a result of a conspiracy over hanging chads.

This is all making Samson rather nervous. It is true that he has the strength of several dozen lions, but ever since Delilah took a pair of scissors to his hair, he hasn't been feeling quite himself. Therefore, he decides that he needs to do something to ensure that the townspeople aren't in a position to replace him. Democracy is all well and good, but there is such a thing as taking things too far.

The plan he comes up with involves the town's only barber. As is well-known, hairy people are exceedingly strong. They're a bit like bears in that respect. So Samson decides to establish a town ordinance that decrees that all the townspeople have to be clean-shaven. Not a hair must remain anywhere on any citizen's head (except on his own, of course).

The law he establishes is formulated as follows: Everybody in Zorah must be clean-shaven, achieving this state of affairs either (a) by shaving themselves; or (b) by visiting the barber to be shaved. In order to save the barber from overwork, no person may shave themselves and also visit the barber.

It seems to Samson that his plan is foolproof. All the townsfolk will be entirely hair-free, which means that despite the best efforts of Delilah, he'll be the hairiest, and therefore, strongest person in Zorah. His power is secure.

He is rather taken aback, then, when the barber flees town under the cover of darkness as soon as the new town ordinance is introduced.

Why did the barber flee town?

SOLUTION ON PAGE 87

VALID OR INVALID?

Sociologist, Alex Gibbon, has been fired from his professorship at North Bovey Institute of Technology after he founded Occupy Bovey — Today Bovey, Tomorrow the World! — and led an ill-fated occupation of the Institute's Senior Common Room. His revolutionary ardour burns as brightly as ever, of course, but he has come to the realisation that if he wants to continue to enjoy his daily Frappuccino, he's going to have to get a job.

This idea doesn't quite fill him with horror — the working classes are noble and true, after all — but he is a little disturbed to find that the *Greater Bovey Gazette* doesn't tend to carry many job adverts for radical lawyers or campaigning journalists. However, his attention has been captured this week by a full-page spread taken out by the Bailey Winepol law offices.

Vacancy — Legal Assistant
Pass the Test Below, We'll Interview You!

Gibbon is intrigued. Although he doesn't see himself as assistant material, he does need a job and the test he has to pass to secure an interview seems straightforward enough. Its instructions are as follows:

For the three arguments below, decide if the given conclusion follows logically from the premises. Answer YES if, and only if, the conclusion can be derived unequivocally from the given premises. Otherwise, answer NO.

	PREMISE	PREMISE	CONCLUSION
ARGUMENT 1	All things that are smoked are good for the health	All cigarettes are smoked	Cigarettes are good for the health
ARGUMENT 2	All animals with four legs are dangerous	Poodles are not dangerous	Poodles are not animals with four legs
ARGUMENT 3	All unemployed people are poor	Donald Trump is not unemployed	Donald Trump is not poor

What answer should Alex Gibbon give for each argument in order to secure an interview?

SOLUTION ON PAGE 89

WHAT WILL THE CROCODILE DO?

Arch-criminal Dave 'The Crocodile' Dundee is wrestling with his conscience. He recently began taking an online ethics course, and it turns out that some of his favourite hobbies, such as throwing fat men off bridges, are ruled out on the grounds of 'Kantian considerations'. He's also learned that profiting at the expense of other people's happiness is out as well. As his whole business model was based on this notion, this has rather thrown him, and left him with the pressing issue of what to do about his latest business endeavour.

He has kidnapped the daughter of local magnet magnate, Ronald Plump. It had been his plan to ransom her off, but he's now feeling torn. On the one hand, he likes money, fast cars and Persian cats; but on the other hand, he has Kant to worry about. He thinks for a while, consults his course notes and comes up with a plan.

He phones Plump and makes him the following offer: if Plump is able to predict correctly whether or not The Crocodile is going to return his daughter, then he'll return her unharmed without a ransom payment. If Plump's prediction is incorrect, then he'll have to pay to get her back.

What prediction should Plump make? And how will The Crocodile respond?

SOLUTION ON PAGE 91

QUICKIE 3

Name three consecutive days without using the words
Monday, Tuesday, Wednesday, Thursday, Friday,
Saturday, or Sunday.

What are the three days?

(SOLUTIONS ON PAGE 140)

QUICKIE 4

AHED is to THA as DAHN is to…

a) PCREE b) DLAER c) VOLGE d) BEREN e) SORAL

WHAT'S GOING ON WITH THE ANDROIDS?

The 100 androids who have made Westworld their home are becoming increasingly frustrated about their inability to enjoy a nice evening out at their local bar, El Santa, on a Thursday night. The android-only bar is quite small, which means that if 60 or more of the androids show up at the same time, then none of them will enjoy themselves. Fewer than 60, though, and they party on, regaling each other with tales of how drunk they would get if only they weren't androids and therefore immune to the effects of alcohol.

The problem on a Thursday night, which is always a *Kraftwerk* theme night, is that either all of the androids show up or none of them show up. They can't seem to get it into their heads that it's not a good idea if they all do exactly the same thing.

The owner of El Santa has decided that things really can't carry on like this, so he calls in local android expert, Noonen Song, to see if he can get to the bottom of matters. Song quickly discovers two facts about the behaviour of the androids that seem to be relevant to the case.

1. The androids have been programmed so that they are not able to discuss with each other whether they are going to visit the bar on any given night (a safety feature introduced after a prearranged bar brawl ended with a small nuclear explosion);
2. The androids decide whether or not to go to the bar on a Thursday evening at exactly the same point in time.

From these two facts, Song is able to deduce why the androids behave in such a peculiar manner. However, as he explains to El Santa's owner, altering their behaviour will be a little problematic.

What has Song deduced about the behaviour of the androids?

SOLUTION ON PAGE 93

2

IS YOUR NEIGHBOR A ZOMBIE?

Man is a credulous animal, and must believe something; in the absence of good grounds for belief, he will be satisfied with bad ones.
BERTRAND RUSSELL

Charles Bowen, a 19th century man of the law, once characterised a metaphysician as 'a blind man in a dark room, looking for a black cat, which isn't there.' In a similar vein, Voltaire, the great Enlightenment thinker, described metaphysics in these terms:

> When he to whom one speaks does not understand, and he who speaks himself does not understand, that is metaphysics.

It is perhaps no surprise, therefore, that metaphysics (which very broadly speaking refers to the study of ultimate reality) throws up its fair share of logical and philosophical conundrums. This chapter features five such conundrums, dealing with issues to do with free will and determinism, personal identity and the problem of other minds. Here there are no easy answers – the issues highlighted by the puzzles featured in this chapter are very much part of ongoing debates.

IS YOUR NEIGHBOR A ZOMBIE?

Jorge Romerio has a perplexing problem. He has recently moved to Sunnyvale, California, but his new neighbors – a strange bunch of would-be ghost hunters – seem to have got it into their heads that he is a zombie. He doesn't look much like a zombie and certainly he doesn't behave like one, but nevertheless they believe him to be one. This is rather disturbing, since there are rumours flying around that Jorge's neighbors have taken to expressing their disdain for all things ectoplasmic by rushing about after dark sticking large chunks of wood into anything that has a whiff of the supernatural about it.

Jorge arranges to meet his ghost-hunting neighbors to explain that he is not a zombie, but rather he is a retired estate agent from rural Pennsylvania. The meeting turns out to be as troubling as the thought that the undead might be making a living buying and selling houses.

The ghost hunters explain that zombies are physically identical to human beings. If you examine their brains you will find all the structures and functionality that make human beings rational, decision-makers. The behaviour of zombies is also identical to that of human beings: just as we live in families, go to work, play sports and watch television, so do zombies. If you stab a zombie, it will cry out in pain. If a zombie's wife dies, then it will exhibit grieving behaviour. As far as it is possible to tell, zombies are identical to humans.

However, there is one crucial difference between zombies and humans. Zombies are dead inside. They have zero consciousness — no thoughts, feelings or awareness. It seems as if they have experiences, emotions, feel pleasure, pain, and so on, and they behave as if they do, but in fact they do not.

The ghost hunters then say that they have been informed by Sunnyvale's resident zombie expert and school librarian, that Jorge is indeed a zombie. However, before eviscerating him, they give him the chance to convince them that he is not.

What should Jorge say to his neighbors to convince them that he has a conscious mind?

RESPONSE ON PAGE 95

CAN YOU BE RESPONSIBLE
FOR WHAT IS UNAVOIDABLE?

John 'Goldtooth' Bentham, evil genius and recent escapee from police custody, has successfully completed yet another dastardly scheme. It had come to his attention that there was a plan afoot to assassinate Bunny Amore, the leader of the radical animal rights group 'Free All Fluffies'. Goldtooth has a strong dislike of anything four-legged; however, because of his recent difficulties with the law, he didn't want to become directly involved, so he proceeded as follows.

He kidnapped the would-be assassin, Boris Huntington, and planted a microchip in his head by means of which he would be able to monitor and control Huntington's actions.

He then wiped Huntington's memory of the kidnapping and surgery, and placed him back in his normal environment, which allowed the plan to proceed as it would have done anyway.

Finally, he used a sophisticated computer program to track Huntington's intentions. If Huntington had shown any sign of diverting from his plan, Goldtooth would have activated the microchip in order to ensure that Huntington went ahead with the assassination.

As it happened, Huntington never did show any sign that

he was having doubts about his plan and the assassination went ahead without Goldtooth having to interfere.

The following things are true about these events:

1. The killing of Bunny Amore was morally wrong;
2. Boris Huntington killed Amore entirely of his own volition: the microchip had no effect whatsoever;
3. There was never any doubt that Huntington was going to attempt to kill Amore – had he wavered, Goldtooth would have activated the microchip.

Is Boris Huntington morally responsible for the act of killing Bunny Amore?

RESPONSE ON PAGE 97

IS TOM PEARCE TOM PEARCE?

It's the 23rd century, and the nature of travel has changed. Tom Pearce, who is travelling to Lesser Bovey today, can just hop into a teletransporter, press a few buttons and he'll pop out a few seconds later at the replicator station in Bovey.

First, he'll step into a scanner, which will record the precise state of every molecule in his body and then destroy his body. A replicator at Bovey will receive this data and create an identical copy of his body. The person who walks out of the replicator will think like Tom Pearce, look like Tom Pearce and believe he is Tom Pearce. He will report that what he experienced was gently falling asleep in the teletransporter, and then immediately waking up in the replicator.

Most people happily use teletransporter technology, but a few people refuse on the grounds that it is not safe. They believe that once the teletransporter destroys a person's body, then that person is dead. The person that emerges at the other end is somebody else — merely a ghastly replica.

Tom Pearce scoffs at such a notion. He has teletransported many times, and nothing untoward has ever occurred to him.

Will Tom survive today's trip to Lesser Bovey?

RESPONSE ON PAGE 99

QUICKIE 5

On what seems to be a normal evening, Ted and Alice are
sitting together in their front room. Ted is watching DVDs,
while Alice is reading *The Time Traveller's Wife*. Suddenly, for
no apparent reason, the power goes out. Ted curses,
and then decides to go to bed. But Alice declines
to follow him. With no use of artificial light, and
in the pitch-dark, she keeps on reading.

How?

(SOLUTIONS ON PAGE 140)

QUICKIE 6

Your current salary is £250 per week. Your boss is feeling
generous, so he increases it by 4%, and then gives you an
additional £8 on top of that.

What's your new salary?

WHAT'S MY POTENTIAL?

It's 1970 and David 'Moonchild' Bread is facing a troubling dilemma. He is desperate to become a father, yet so far has refrained from engaging in sexual relations with women on the grounds that he doesn't want to be in a situation where he has to take off his favourite kaftan. So, feeling a little less than groovy, he trots off to the Citizens Advice Bureau for some life counselling.

The advice he gets there is simple:

ADVISOR: *Look here, Moonchild, there's at least the potential you'll become a father if you have sex with a few women, but if you don't, then there isn't. You've got to get yourself out there: you know, put yourself in the game. That's if you want children. If not, you could always relocate to an ashram and devote your life to Himalayan goat herding.*

The having lots of sex aspect of this advice seems sage to Moonchild, so he spends the next 40 years having as much sex, with as many different women, as untamed facial hair and a kaftan that eventually becomes sculpted to his body allows.

However, fortune doesn't smile upon him, and he doesn't manage to beget a single child, so he returns to the Citizens Advice Bureau in a huff, where, by some strange quirk of fate, the original advisor is still working (such are the perks of a public sector job). Moonchild – now calling himself 'Ice Moon' – gets straight to the point.

ICE MOON: *Hey, you said I had the potential to be a father. I've wasted 40 years of my life having endless sex with women when it's obvious I never had that potential!*

The following things are true: Moonchild is not infertile; he did have sex with many, many women; it was often the case that no contraception was used; he has never fathered a child.

Did Moonchild ever have the potential to be a father?

RESPONSE ON PAGE 101

WHO GETS TORTURED?

Kassandra Hedges and Susannah Mills have spent their gap year touring the Internet cafés of the great Amazon Basin. Unfortunately, patronising the indigenous peoples of South America has ended up costing them more than they expected, which means they have run out of money. In an attempt to rectify their impecuniousness, the two girls have responded to an advert that promises riches in return for their participation in a medical trial. Trouble is, it turns out this is no ordinary medical trial.

David Jared, a technician at Methuselah labs, explains to Kassandra and Susannah that he and his colleagues are in the process of developing a new technology that will allow the contents of a brain to be transferred into a new body. He tells them that the trial for which they have so recklessly signed up will proceed as follows:

First, Kassandra's thoughts, memories and dispositions will be extracted from her brain, which will then be wiped clean so that all the information that was previously stored there is erased. At exactly the same time, the same thing will happen to Susannah.

Next, Kassandra's thoughts, memories and dispositions will be transferred into the brain that previously contained Susannah's thoughts, memories and dispositions (and which is still in the body Susannah had been calling her own); and Susannah's thoughts, memories and dispositions will be transferred in the same way, but in the opposite direction.

It is at this point that things will take a rather sinister turn. David explains that in order to check that the pain and pleasure centres of the two brains are still working after the procedure, one of the two girls will given a $1,000,000 reward, and the other girl will be tortured. He tells Kassandra that she gets to choose which of the two girls will be rewarded and who will be tortured.

Assuming that it is inevitable somebody will be tortured and that Kassandra doesn't want it to be her (i.e. she's going to choose selfishly), she must choose between the body that used to be hers, but now contains Susannah's thoughts, memories and dispositions (hereafter Body-Person A) and the body that used to belong to Susannah, but now contains her own thoughts, memories and dispositions (hereafter Body-Person B).

Who should Kassandra choose to be tortured?

RESPONSE ON PAGE 103

3

WHAT IF MONTY DOESN'T KNOW?

Take away paradox from the thinker and you have a professor.
SØREN KIERKEGAARD

There are a number of paradoxes and puzzles that are rightly considered to be classics of their kind. The trolley problem, Zeno's paradoxes, the Monty Hall problem, and the prisoner's dilemma, all spring to mind.

This chapter features four such classic puzzles. A couple are variations on two original classics – the Monty Hall problem and the trolley problem, respectively. The other two are classics in their own right, albeit they are dressed up in fancy clothing for their appearance here.

You'll be pleased to hear that at least some of the puzzles featured in this chapter have right answers. However, you should also note that the variation on the Monty Hall problem that appears here is particularly tricky, so don't feel too bad if you struggle to follow its logic.

WHAT IF MONTY DOESN'T KNOW?

William Capra can't believe his luck. Having already appeared on *Ferrari or Goat*, television's number one game show, during which he was lucky enough to secure ownership of a slightly moth-eaten goat, he has now been invited back. The game has the following form:

There are three doors. Behind one door is a brand new Ferrari, behind the other two, goats. The goats and the Ferrari have been randomly allocated to their respective doors. William must choose one door. The game show host, Monty Hall, who knows what is behind the doors, will then open one of the two remaining doors and he has to reveal a goat. William, who desperately wants to win the Ferrari, must then decide whether to stick with his original choice, or to switch to the remaining unopened door.

William is feeling confident because he knows in this game the right strategy is to switch his choice. The only circumstance in which he doesn't win if he switches is if he originally picked the door with the car behind it. There is a one in three chance that he originally picked the door with the car, and therefore a one in three chance he won't win if he switches his choice. This means, of course, that there's a two in three chance he will win if he does switch. He should, therefore, switch.

The game starts with a televisual flourish. William chooses his door: Door 1. Then, disaster strikes. As Monty Hall goes to open a door (with the intention of revealing a

goat), he slips on a stray goat dropping, flies through the air, and inadvertently bashes into Door 3, which crashes open revealing... a somewhat startled goat. This is purely a matter of luck: Monty had no control over the direction of his fall, and it was just as likely he would have bashed into Door 2, revealing whatever is behind it instead.

After recovering his composure, and placating the goat, Monty decides that the show must go on. But things have now changed subtly. Monty only revealed the goat by chance. So what are the odds of winning if William now switches? Does the fact Monty didn't know what he'd be revealing alter the calculation?

Should William still switch doors?

RESPONSE ON PAGE 105

SHOULD YOU RUN OVER THE FAT MAN?

Pacey Bones, the world's unluckiest train driver, is at the controls of his locomotive, The Speedy Bullock, when he is informed via his Twitter feed that the recurrence of a design fault means that if he applies the train's brakes before it reaches the next station, it will explode, killing all 500 passengers on board. Something like this has happened to him before, only on the previous occasion there was the added complication that the train was speeding towards five people who were tied to the track between it and the next station. The only way he was able to avoid running them down was by hitting a button that directed the train into a siding track, where unfortunately, it ran over and killed a person who had become glued fast to the track as a result of a stag night accident.

Pacey is just thinking to himself he's lucky he doesn't have to face that complication again, when his CB radio crackles and he's informed that he is once again facing a people on the track situation. Cursing that he seems to be involved in some ridiculous sequel, Casey asks for further details.

He is informed the situation is the same as it was previously only with a subtle complication. The siding track into which he has to divert the train if he wants to avoid running down the five people on the main track loops back onto the main track, which means the train will be sent back up the track towards the five people who will be run down anyway. Ironically, in the loop back situation, the train will reach the station before it reaches the five people, but, given its current speed and momentum, even if Casey hits the brakes as soon as it reaches the station, the train won't stop quickly enough to avoid squashing them.

However, there is a further aspect to the story. Another stag night accident has occurred, and a very fat man has become attached to the siding track. His weight is such that if the train hits him, its speed will be sufficiently reduced so that if Casey brakes as soon as the train reaches the station, it will stop before it reaches the five people tied to the main track and their lives will be saved.

Should Casey press the button to divert the train into the siding?

RESPONSE ON PAGE 108

IS ZEUS LOSING HIS POWER?

Zeus, leader of the Mount Olympus pantheon of gods, is feeling a little fed up. His wife, Hera, has not been herself since she finished reading Betty Friedan's *The Feminine Mystique*. She's taken to staying out late, seems to have struck up an inappropriate relationship with his Italian half-brother, Neptune, and has even on occasion refused to iron his shirts.

Worst of all, though, she has started to question Zeus's godly prowess. Zeus had been boasting about his omnipotence, and joking around that he'd be willing to move mountains for her, and then doing just that, when she asked him whether he had the power to create a mountain that he wouldn't be able to move.

Zeus blustered that he couldn't see why anybody would want to do such a daft thing, but she just smirked, and then asked whether he could create a lock that he couldn't unlock. Zeus stalked off, but the truth is he's not sure whether he can do this sort of thing. It simply hadn't occurred to him before now that there might be a limit to his power.

Is Zeus right to be concerned? Does this mean that he's not omnipotent?

RESPONSE ON PAGE 111

QUICKIE 7

David, Susan, Jack and Jill live together in the same shared
student house. One night, David and Susan go out to
watch a movie. They have a good time, but when they
return, they're devastated to find Jack lying dead in a pool
of water, surrounded by broken glass.

It is obvious that Jill has killed him,
but she is not prosecuted, nor severely punished. Why?

(SOLUTIONS ON PAGE 140)

QUICKIE 8

A car leaves Toronto at 6.20 PM and arrives in Detroit,
180 miles away, at 10.05 PM.

What is its average speed in miles per hour?

IS IT NECESSARILY WRONG TO EAT PEOPLE?

In retrospect, it was perhaps not the wisest move on the part of the Cradock Cookery Club to choose potholing as its team bonding activity. Things had started well enough with a nice cheese luncheon at the entrance to Limburger Gorge, and even a rather heated debate about the relative merits of stalactites versus stalagmites hadn't been enough to dampen spirits as the merry band entered the Hirtenkäse Cavern. However, spirits had taken something of a dive when a vast landslide cut off five club members from the outside world.

It's now 30 days later, and some rather disquieting news has just emerged from the cavern (via a specially installed mobile phone system). Apparently, Lonnie Fuller, one of the trapped club members, has been killed and eaten by his colleagues. This is not a complete surprise: the group had recently been informed that it was vanishingly unlikely they would continue to survive without food for long enough for a rescue to take place. Their response had been to enquire whether their chances would be improved if they consumed the flesh of one of their own number. The medical team on the surface had been extremely reluctant to answer, but had eventually responded in the affirmative.

Prompted by Fuller himself, the group then agreed to draw lots to determine who should be killed and eaten. However, before the draw took place, Fuller had withdrawn from the agreement, saying he wanted to wait a little more time before going ahead. The others, however, went ahead without him and drew a lot on his behalf (having secured Fuller's agreement that the draw was at least fair). The draw went against him and he was killed and eaten.

The question that is now worrying the survivors is whether they'll be charged and convicted of murder if they are rescued. The statute books state: 'Whoever shall willfully take the life of another shall be punished by death.' However, it is overwhelmingly likely that if they hadn't taken Fuller's life then they all would have died. It seems extraordinary to think that they might be rescued and then executed for doing the only thing that had a realistic chance of saving their lives. There is no dispute here about the facts of the case.

Do these facts support a conviction and punishment for the crime of murder?

RESPONSE ON PAGE 113

· What's Going to Happen at the Robber's Cave? · Is Homo Sapiens a
Noble Savage? · Will Help Arrive? · Whom do You Prefer?
· How About a Date? · How Obedient Are We?
· Who Should Lizzy Choose?

4

HOW OBEDIENT ARE WE?

*When a hundred men stand together, each of them loses
his mind and gets another one.*
FRIEDRICH NIETZSCHE

This chapter is a change of pace; rather than asking you to
make sense of some logic puzzle or counterintuitive thought
experiment, you're required to make judgements about how
people will likely react in specific situations.

Thanks to the work of brilliant social psychologists such
as Soloman Asch, Muzafer Sherif, Stanley Milgram, Henri
Tajfel and Elliot Aronson, we understand a great deal of how
human beings behave in particular circumstances. But does
what you think you know about human psychology match
what we actually do know about it?

A word of caution here — human psychology is complex
and social psychology is a young science, so its conclusions
are necessarily tentative. However, this tentativeness is not
always reflected in the language of this chapter — because it's
more fun that way — but should be taken as a given.

WHAT'S GOING TO HAPPEN AT THE ROBBER'S CAVE?

Bill Silverman, Director of Recreational Activities at Robber's Cave National Park, is facing a bit of a dilemma. For the last fifteen years, the park has played host to a boy scout summer camp, which takes the following form:

- The boys, normally numbering around twenty in total, are randomly assigned to two groups.
- During the first week, each group goes off on its own, and then spends time engaged in group activities such as tent pitching, song singing and woggle making.
- At the beginning of the second week, there is a friendly competition between the two groups.
- The competition involves a series of sporting events, plus bonus points awarded to the group with the most pristine tents, best rendition of Kumbaya, and so on.

This has always gone rather well. The boys value the time they spend alone with their groups, but also enjoy the competition, which has always remained friendly. So it's been a very successful annual event over the last fifteen years.

But this year, something is different. In previous years, the boys have always known each other prior to arriving at the camp. As a result, the two groups in competition with each other have always been subordinate to the wider group in terms of the loyalty of the boys. This year there's reason to think this won't be the case. Silverman has been informed that the boys have never met each other before.

This worries Silverman. He's read *Lord of the Flies* often enough to have a good idea what happens when groups of feral youngsters get together. He is slightly consoled by the news that the boys aren't exactly feral, but rather from affluent families, supposedly well-adjusted and doing well in school. But even so, he has images of them whacking each other over the head with stray conches.

Is Silverman right to be worried? On the one hand, we know for certain that things have previously always gone well when the two competing groups are made up of boys who already know each other. On the other hand, we also know that competition and rivalry can lead to hostility.

Will the fact that this time the boys don't know each other beforehand mean that the scout camp will descend into chaos and anarchy?

RESPONSE ON PAGE 116

IS HOMO SAPIENS A NOBLE SAVAGE?

Alex Gibbon, sociologist, Marxist and trainee barista, has only been in his new job at The Cappuccino House for a week and he's already in trouble. In an attempt to raise the political consciousness of its clientele, he has been handing out copies of his self-published pamphlet, *Reclaiming Utopia: Capitalism and the Seeds of Conflict.* Unfortunately, the owner of The Cappucinno House, Carl Hopper, is not impressed by the pamphlet's content. He considers Gibbon's contention that the schisms between human beings are merely a function of material inequality to be hopelessly naive.

According to Gibbon, human beings are essentially good, peaceable and co-operative and it is only the distorting effects of class society that sets them at each other's throats. The glorious communist revolution, which is surely now only a few months away, will return humanity to this happy state, and conflict will be a thing of the past.

Hopper, resisting the temptation of allowing capitalist inequality to cause him to thwack Gibbon with a percolator, argues that Thomas Hobbes got it right. Human beings need barely any excuse to carve up the world into the righteous and the unrighteous, and to do unto each other all manner of mischief and violence.

So who is right?

RESPONSE ON PAGE 118

QUICKIE 9

All mammals are mortal. Women are mortal.
Therefore, women are mammals.

*Is this syllogism valid? Does the conclusion necessarily
follow, if the premises are true?*

(SOLUTIONS ON PAGE 141)

QUICKIE 10

*Which figure above has the longer straight line
(i.e., not including the arrow-heads)?*

WILL HELP ARRIVE?

The renowned bounty hunter, Goldilocks, is on a mission to track down the notorious, Three Bears Massive, a gang that has been terrorising porridge manufacturers throughout the state of Montana. All she knows about the group is that it has three members — according to eyewitnesses, a male, a female and an annoying child — and they are currently thought to be hiding out in the woods of Glacier National Park.

This explains Goldilocks' current, rather worrisome, predicament. She's alone in a tent in the backcountry area of Glacier National Park and she can hear noises. It isn't entirely clear what's responsible for the noises, but she rather suspects it might be large and furry. So far she's heard rustling, the occasional snort and possibly the sound of a Cornflakes box being devoured.

Goldilocks, mindful of the fate of Little Red Riding Hood, contemplates calling for help. Luckily enough, she has pitched her tent in a designated camping area, so there are plenty of other people around. However, she's not entirely convinced that they will come to her aid even if they hear her cries. She vaguely recalls learning about an incident that occurred in New York City, where a young woman was stabbed to death, despite the fact that dozens of people witnessed her murder.

Goldilocks reasons as follows:

- If she calls out, then there's a chance that she'll attract the attention of whatever it is that's causing the noises she can hear outside her tent.
- Therefore, in order for the benefits of calling out to outweigh the risks, she has to be fairly sure that people will come to her aid if they hear her cry out for help.
- She knows that there are people within earshot, but she doesn't know whether they'll help her.

What should Goldilocks do in this situation?
Will people come to her aid if they
hear her calling for help?

RESPONSE ON PAGE 121

WHOM DO YOU PREFER?

Peter Campbell has always been proud of his ability to make judgements about how other people are likely to react to particular events and phenomena. While his friends insisted that only crazy people would appreciate the charms of Jedward, Peter always knew the twins would make it big, and while many thought the Snuggie was just a dressing gown inadvertently worn backwards, Peter knew from the moment he first set eyes on one that it was going to be the next big thing in evening wear.

So he is very pleased when a job comes up that seems particularly suited to his abilities: Chief Spin Doctor at the radical animal rights group, 'Free All Fluffies'. Unfortunately, Lapin Amore, Director of Human Resources at Free All Fluffies, won't give Peter the job without him successfully completing the following test.

Group A and Group B both comprise 20 people. Each group is required to make a judgement about a further person, Zach Coine, based on a description of that person made up of just six words. Peter's job is to predict what sort of judgement each group will make, and in particular whether they will judge the person positively or negatively.

Group A
Intelligent – Industrious – Impulsive – Critical –
Stubborn – Envious

Group B

Envious — Stubborn — Critical — Impulsive —
Industrious — Intelligent

Peter can hardly believe his luck when he sees the two sets of words. It seems obvious to him that Zach Coine 1 is a much more sympathetic character than Zach Coine 2, and consequently that he will be judged more positively. Zach Coine 1 appears to be a go-getter, who knows what he wants and pursues it assiduously. Zach Coine 2, on the other hand, seems almost certain to let his good qualities, such as industry and intelligence, be trumped by his jealousy and stubbornness, and therefore he is surely much less likely to be successful in what he does.

Is Peter right to predict that Group A will judge Zach Coine more positively than Group B?

RESPONSE ON PAGE 123

HOW ABOUT A DATE?

Jerry Chow, president of the Society for the Promotion of Ugly People (SPUP), is having an argument with his mother about the wisdom of attending Prohibition, a burlesque themed night at Bella Donna, a premier nightclub on the Humberside Riviera.

JERRY: *Come on, you're not really trying to tell me that I'm going to look good in tassels and a feather boa...*

MOTHER: *Well, that's not an image I care to contemplate. What I'm telling you is that physical attractiveness isn't everything.*

JERRY: *So you're saying I'm ugly?!*

MOTHER: *I prefer the term 'homely' and anyway you're the president of SPUP, so spare me the indignation. I'm just saying that if you go along to your event and let your personality shine through, then some young lady is going to take a fancy to you. You're a funny guy.*

JERRY: *I'm 5 ft 2 in.*

MOTHER: *You're 5 ft 1 in. But people just aren't as shallow as you suppose. Do you really think you're going to be dismissed just because you resemble a bad-tempered goblin? You have a beautiful soul. You're caring, compassionate, you love goats; these are all things that people find attractive. Go to your dance, talk to people, be yourself, and then if you make a connection with somebody, ask them out.*

JERRY: *Sorry, but you're just vastly underestimating the importance of physical attractiveness. If you're unattractive, then you're less likely to be thought of as intelligent, warm, well-adjusted and competent. There's even evidence that you'll do less well in your career than your better looking colleagues. Did you know that every US president elected between 1900 and 1968 was taller than his major opponent?*

MOTHER: *Oh lord, not this again. I've read the SPUP literature, dear. It doesn't alter the fact that homely looking people go on dates! Put on your tassels, go to Bella Donna, and ask out a young lady. I'll bet she says yes!*

Is Jerry's mother correct to think that attractiveness is about more than just physical appearance? Or is beauty really only skin deep?

RESPONSE ON PAGE 125

HOW OBEDIENT ARE WE?

David Jared, one-time technician at Methuselah labs, is on trial for terrible crimes. He has been transplanting the brains of young backpackers as part of some kind of strange brain swap experiment and then proceeding to torture half of the people who underwent the operation (though lawyers can't quite agree on exactly who was tortured).

Jared does not deny these things, but claims he should be shown leniency, because the vast majority of people in his situation would have behaved in the same way. It was simply part of his job to carry out the transplants and to inflict torture upon people; he was obeying orders.

He is asked in court why he didn't refuse to carry out the instructions given to him. He responds that at the time everything seemed to be above board. His superiors were highly qualified scientists, the victims had signed consent forms and the facilities within which he was working were modern and hi-tech. He now sees that his confidence was misplaced, but asserts that his behaviour was no different than most other people's would have been.

Would most people be willing to torture another human being if instructed to do so in these sorts of circumstances?

RESPONSE ON PAGE 127

QUICKIE 11

Five percent of people living in Chicago have unlisted
telephone numbers.

*Suppose you select 150 numbers at random from the
city's phone directory, how many of the people selected
will have unlisted phone numbers?*

(SOLUTIONS ON PAGE 141)

QUICKIE 12

Mary is 32 years old.
She is four times as old as her brother.

*How old will Mary be when
she is twice as old as her brother?*

WHO SHOULD LIZZY CHOOSE?

Lizzy Bennett, a contestant on the hit television show, *The Spouse Factor*, has to make a decision that might change her life. In front of a studio and live television audience, she has to choose the man she hopes to make her husband.

The television show has the following format. Three people of the same sex and one person of the opposite sex, all of whom are unattached and looking for a spouse, perform a series of tasks and answer a number of questions that enable the studio audience and viewers at home to rank them across a number of dimensions, including, for example, attractiveness, intelligence, resourcefulness and sense of humour.

This information is then provided to the single male or female contestant, who is encouraged to use the rankings data to help them choose which of the three people of the opposite sex they want to accompany on a romantic holiday. They have ten minutes to make their choice, during which time they can interact with the three people they're choosing between (albeit they can't actually see them).

Lizzy's dilemma is as follows. On the basis of her conversations with the three male contestants, she prefers 'Charlie' to both 'William' and 'George'. However, the rankings data tells her that Charlie scores better than she does across a whole range of dimensions, including attractiveness, intelligence and charisma. William, on the other hand, who seems to her perfectly pleasant, matches her scores almost completely.

Not surprisingly, Lizzy is inclined to choose Charlie. He is clearly the preferred contestant and she's not immune to the appeal of a good-looking, charismatic man. But she can't help wondering whether perhaps William would be the better bet for a lasting relationship, which is what she wants to get out of her appearance on *The Spouse Factor*. To put it simply, her worry is that Charlie is a little bit out of her league. She suspects that it is nonsense to think about relationships in this sort of way, especially since she doesn't really have much information to go on, but she does want to maximise her chances of establishing a long-term match.

Who should Lizzy choose if her aim is to find somebody to love over the long-term?

RESPONSE ON PAGE 129

· Is it Rational to Believe in Monsters Under the Bed?
· When is a Belief Not a Belief? · Are We Brains in Vats?
· Did We Evolve to Know About the World?

5

WHEN IS A BELIEF NOT A BELIEF?

*To know, is to know that you know nothing. That is the
meaning of true knowledge.*
SOCRATES

Perhaps the most irksome of philosophical problems is that
posed by radical scepticism about the possibility of
knowledge. In essence, radical scepticism asserts that since
we don't have unmediated access to the external world, and
since we cannot rule out that we are in certain ways
systematically deceived about the nature of reality, we cannot
claim to have knowledge of the world.

The puzzles and conundrums featured in this chapter
explore the limits of knowledge and belief. If you're able
to find solutions here, then you've succeeded where some
of the greatest minds in history over the last 2,000 years
have failed. Clearly, in this situation, you should
immediately give up your day job, and become a
philosopher. This will likely result in a drop in income,
but your renown will be guaranteed.

IS IT RATIONAL TO BELIEVE IN MONSTERS UNDER THE BED?

Boris Stokes considers himself a logical sort of fellow. He's a member of his local Skeptics Society, enjoys the odd game of Sudoku and even owned a chemistry set when he was younger. But unfortunately, he has recently been experiencing what he takes to be hallucinations. Nothing pleasant either, but rather a large monster with very sharp teeth. He knows that no such monsters exist in the real world so he visits a psychiatrist who tells him that it's either a sane reaction to an insane world or he has a mental illness.

Boris is well aware that hallucinations can occur because of disturbances in the brain so he tends towards the view he has a mental illness. He certainly doesn't believe the monster exists, although it is disconcerting that he experiences it as being as real and as solid as any of the other objects — tables, chairs, and the like — in his world.

Boris decides the best thing to do is just to ignore the monster and carry on with his life on the (rationally justified) assumption that it does not exist. This works well for a while, but then things begin to change. The monster becomes more aggressive: it begins to snarl in Boris's direction and pinch the remote control when he wants to watch *90210*. Not surprisingly, Boris isn't best pleased by this turn of events. Yes, the monster might just be an hallucination, but what happens if it attacks? It's possible that it would hurt every bit as much as it would were it actually a real monster. And there is this nagging thought:

suppose the monster is real? Boris realises there are no monsters, but they're not ruled out as a matter of logic. There could be monsters.

And then it happens. It's late at night. Boris is alone in his bathroom when the monster comes crashing in through the window — at least this is what Boris experiences — and it's on him. It doesn't immediately attack, but it's right in his face and he can smell rotting flesh on its breath. Boris closes his eyes and wills the monster to disappear, but he can hear its breathing and sense its malevolence and in his head there's this insistent thought: What if it's real? So the question then is this:

Is it reasonable in this situation for Boris to accept that the monster is real and to take evasive action?

RESPONSE ON PAGE 131

WHEN IS A BELIEF NOT A BELIEF?

David and Nicola are hopelessly in love with each other. They spend their days, as do all loving couples, gazing longingly into each other's eyes, emailing photos of kittens to each other, and monitoring each other's Facebook accounts for inappropriate flirting behaviour. However, there is one rather large cloud threatening to disrupt this romantic idyll – namely, death. It's not that either of them is planning to die anytime soon, but they are aware that their love cannot last forever, a fact which is making them increasingly anxious.

It is a happy surprise, then, when one evening as they're about to enjoy a Babycham or two in their local hostelry, an angel called Jim appears before them and offers them the following deal. If they split up for 20 years, and have no contact with each other, he'll fix it so they spend eternity together. A little taken aback by this offer, they ask Jim the Angel to fill in some of the details.

He explains that it is a one-shot deal, which has two strict conditions:

1. If they accept, then not only will they be separated for 20 years, but it will be impossible for them to contact each other.
2. Having made their decision, they will be unable to change their minds.

The good news, though, is that the deal also comes with the following guarantees:

1. They will spend eternity together.
2. They will be blissfully happy together and will never come to regret their decision.
3. Although they will have no contact with each other for 20 years, they will not be fundamentally altered by their time apart.

Jim is an angel, so David and Nicola are certain he is telling the truth. They are also clear in their own minds that they want to spend the rest of time together. However, they aren't sure whether they should accept his deal. The compensation of eternity together is a significant reward. But they will miss each other during the time they're apart, so it's not something they'd undertake lightly.

Should they accept the deal? If they accept the deal, how should they feel on parting from each other?

RESPONSE ON PAGE 133

ARE WE BRAINS IN VATS?

Hugo Smith is operations manager at a Brain-In-A-Vat farm, where human brains exist in a vat of life-sustaining fluid, connected to a simulation device that replicates electrical impulses from the outside world, creating a virtual reality that is indistinguishable from the real world.

Hugo manages 'Free Thoughts Farm', which comprises many thousands of individual brains in a vat, each one being fed a perfect simulation of life in Cleveland, Ohio. Or so he thought until a conversation he had this morning. As he was about to tuck into his Bran Flakes, a man named Orpheus explained that he's not working at the farm at all, but rather he is himself a brain in a vat, currently being fed electrical impulses by a supercomputer in Folkestone, England.

Of course, this all struck Hugo as being rather far-fetched, especially when Orpheus started going on about different coloured pills, but Hugo is now a little worried. He has no particular reason to suspect that Orpheus was telling the truth, but he's aware that this is also precisely what he'd think if he were living in a simulated reality.

How can Hugo be sure that he is not merely a brain in a vat experiencing a virtual reality?

RESPONSE ON PAGE 136

QUICKIE 13

You're going to the theatre and you're paying for tickets.

Would it be cheaper to take one friend to the theatre twice (assuming the cost of tickets remains the same) or two friends to the theatre at the same time?

QUICKIE 14

Two elderly people wish to cross a river. The only way to get across the river is by boat. The boat can only take one person at a time. There is no way the boat can travel without a passenger, and there are no ropes or anything else of that nature available.

Despite all this, the two elderly people are able to get across the river. How?

DID WE EVOLVE TO KNOW ABOUT THE WORLD?

The three members of the notorious Three Bears Massive are discussing the curious ways of human beings, while tucking into a lovely meal of Cornflakes, tent and a currently unidentified meat substance.

The bears start by affirming their commitment to a Darwinian conception of the human species. As far as they are concerned, human beings, like themselves, are a product of evolution by natural selection. Humans might have bigger brains than bears — though they find this hard to believe in the case of Little Red Riding Hood — but human brains are still purely physical entities that process data from the outside world via their sense organs. Brains are built according to the instructions provided by genes; the genes that result in brains that successfully facilitate reproduction will be passed on more often than their less successful alternatives. The bears are thoroughly naturalistic in their outlook, being convinced that this whole process is driven by determinate physical laws.

It is partly for this reason they find human beings a little puzzling. Humans seem to be interested in finding things out about the world — in what they call 'knowledge' and 'truth'. So, for example, rather than being content merely to eat honey, they are curious to find out about its

constituent elements and how it is produced. However, given that human brains evolved through entirely naturalistic processes, it isn't at all clear that brains are suited to this task. In Darwinian terms, the task of brains is to facilitate survival, not to construct accurate representations of the world. Natural selection isn't interested in the truth, in and of itself, merely in rewarding whatever it is that facilitates reproduction.

The bears are also aware that there is a huge unsolved puzzle lurking around here: how it is possible for physical things to know anything at all? Or, to put this in the pungent terms of the philosopher, Colin McGinn, how it is that 'meat' can know anything at all?

Is it right to think there is a tension between the naturalistic origins of the brain and the belief that humans are able to find out the truth about things?

RESPONSE ON PAGE 138

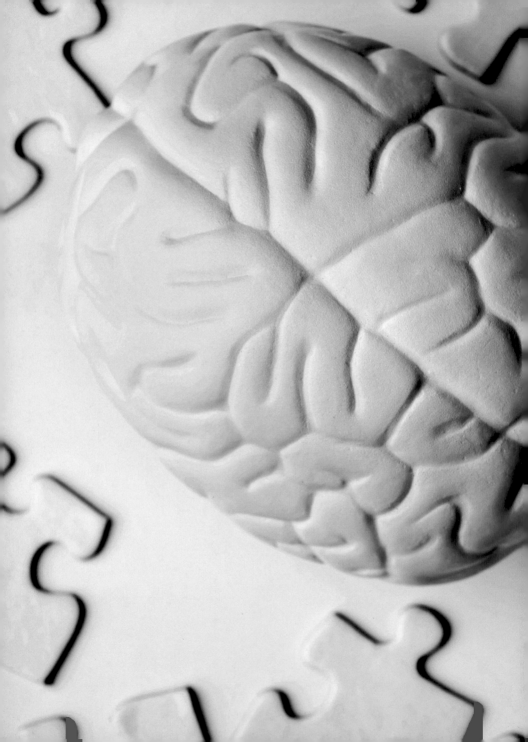

SOLUTIONS

RED BALL OR GREEN BALL?

(see pages 10–11)

The answer is that it makes no difference which urn is chosen since the probability of a red ball being drawn from either urn is 1 in 2 (50%).

This is obviously true in the case of Urn B, since there are 100 balls in total, of which 50 are red (50/100 = 1/2). It is also true in the case of Urn A, despite the fact the precise number of red balls it contains is unknown, though the reason it's true is a little more complex.

In the case of Urn A, we know that all combinations of red and green balls are equally likely. This means that the probability that Urn A will contain (50 − n) red balls is identical to the probability that it will contain (50 + n) red balls (where n is any number between 0 and 50). The ns here cancel each other out, leaving an overall probability of 50 out of 100 (or 1 in 2).

If that's not clear, then it might help to think in terms of particular numbers: so, for example, the probability that the urn will contain 49 red balls is identical to the probability that it will contain 51 red balls; the probability of 48 red balls is the same as it is for 52 red balls; and and so on.

The Ambiguity Effect

As it stands, this is just a fairly simple probability calculation. However, what's interesting about this sort of puzzle is that people tend to respond to them in terms of what has been called the ambiguity effect. First described by economist, Daniel Ellsberg, this refers to the fact that people will normally choose the option where the probability of selecting the winning ball is known, even though it affords no greater chance of winning overall. Or, to put this another way, people will normally shy away from the 'ambiguous' option, despite the fact it offers the same chance of a favourable outcome as the option where the probabilities are known. In our scenario, this means that most people will choose Urn B.

Equal Outcomes

This effect is strong enough to lead people to make choices that are on the face of it nonsensical. Consider, for example, the following variation on the scenario involving Frank and the red balls.

We'll assume that he chose Urn B as the urn from which the first ball should be drawn, and that the ball turned out to be red. The urn is then replenished with another red ball (so the situation is exactly as it was originally), and Frank is told to choose again. However, this time in order to borrow a red ball for the evening – the favourable outcome from Frank's point of view – a green ball must be drawn from one of the urns. So given this setup, which urn should Frank choose?

The answer again is that it makes no difference. However, what is curious about this variation is that in this situation most people will still choose Urn B even though they're now hoping for the opposite outcome. But this makes very little sense. We know that the ratio of red to green balls in Urn B is 50:50. Therefore, it follows that the only reason for originally favouring Urn B over Urn A was the belief that there was a less than 50% chance that a red ball would be drawn from Urn A (otherwise there is no advantage in choosing Urn B).

From this it also follows that the original choice implies a belief that there was a greater than 50% chance that a green ball would be drawn from Urn A (remember, there are only red and green balls in the urns). However, this means that when it comes to making the second choice, where the favourable outcome is a green ball, it makes very little sense, if any at all, to choose Urn B again. We know the chance of drawing a green ball from Urn B is 50% (1 in 2), which, as we have seen, is less than what must originally have been believed to be the probability of drawing a green ball from Urn A.

IS THE ELEVATOR MALFUNCTIONING?

(see pages 12–13)

(see pages 12–13)

This is a version of a puzzle, first described by physicists Marvin Stern and George Gamow, termed the Elevator Paradox. The key to understanding what's going on here is the respective locations of Peter and Eloise's apartments. Peter's apartment is on the next to bottom floor; Eloise's apartment is on the next to top floor. This means that the elevator will tend to be travelling downwards at the point at which Peter want to embark, and upwards at the point at which Eloise wants to. Here's why.

In basic terms, the explanation is simple. The elevator will spend the vast majority of its time above the level of Peter's floor, so the chances are it will be above him when he arrives at the elevator door, which means it'll be travelling downwards the first time he sees it. It's the other way around for Eloise: the elevator will spend most of its time beneath the level of her floor, so it will tend to be below her when she wants to catch it, which means it'll be travelling upwards the first time she sees it.

The follow example should make this clear. Imagine a ten storey building where the elevator takes two minutes between each floor. The table on the next page shows how the timing of the elevator looks starting at 7:58 in the morning.

As you can see, it takes a total of 36 minutes for the elevator to complete a round-trip. The key point here is that if you live on the next to bottom floor – i.e., the 1st floor – then you need to arrive at the elevator during a precise four-minute window in order for the elevator to be heading upwards when you first see it – specifically, you need to arrive between 7:58 and 8:02. If you arrive at any other time during the 36 minutes, the first elevator you see is going to be travelling downwards. It follows, then, that if you arrive at some random time between 7:58 and 8:34, it's much more likely that the first elevator you see will be travelling downwards rather than upwards (which, of course, is precisely what Peter experiences).

In the real world, there are variables that complicate this picture. For example, it's likely that an elevator will tend to idle on the ground floor, which will increase the chance an elevator will be travelling upwards when you first see it. Nevertheless, in a single elevator building, this basic pattern will play out. If you live near the ground floor, then more often than not the first elevator you see will be heading downwards. If you live near the top floor, it will tend to be the other way around.

Floor	Time
1st Floor	7.58
Ground Floor	8.00
1st Floor	8.02
2nd Floor	8.04
3rd Floor	8.06
4th Floor	8.08
5th Floor	8.10
6th Floor	8.12
7th Flloor	8.14
8th Floor	8.16
9th Floor	8.18
8th Floor	8.20
7th Floor	8.22
6th Floor	8.24
5th Floor	8.26
4th Floor	8.28
3rd Floor	8.30
2ndFloor	8.32
1st Floor	8.34
Ground Floor	8.36

WHAT COLOUR IS YOUR RAVEN?

Hard though it is to believe, it is possible that the existence of a red apple does support the claim that all ravens are black. To understand why, it is necessary to consider what is known as the Raven Paradox, which was first proposed by German logician, Carl Gustav Hempel, in the 1940s.

The argument to follow is a little complex, but if we take it slowly, it should be possible to get clear about it. The best starting point is to note that the proposition, 'all ravens are black' is logically equivalent to the proposition, 'everything that is not black is not a raven'.

Logical Equivalency

To understand why this is the case, consider what necessarily follows from the truth or falsity of the second of these propositions. If it is true that everything that is not black is not a raven, then it must also be true that all ravens are black, since there are no non-black things that are ravens. If, on the other hand, it is false that everything that is not black is not a raven, then it must also be false that all ravens are black, since there is at least one non-black thing that is a raven. Put these two things together, and you've got logical equivalency.

The next stage in the argument is to consider what counts as evidence in support of the first proposition. In this regard, it seems obviously true that if you observe an instance of a black raven then that would count as evidence in support of the claim that 'all ravens are black'. It doesn't demonstrate its truth, of course, but nevertheless the existence of even a single black raven certainly seems to count in favour of the proposition.

If it is true of 'all ravens are black' that a single observable instance that conforms to the proposition counts as evidence in its favour, then presumably it must also be true of 'everything that is not black is not a raven'. In other words, if we can find a single instance of a thing that is not black and not a raven, then it seems that this must count as evidence in favour of the truth of the proposition. A red apple is such a thing, of course, since it is neither black, nor a raven. It follows, therefore, that the existence of a red apple is evidence in support of the claim that 'everything that is not black is not a raven.'

Closing Argument

This leads us to the final move in the argument. We noted earlier that the proposition 'all ravens are black' is logically equivalent to the proposition 'everything that is not black is not a raven'. This means that if a red apple is evidence in favour of latter proposition, it must also be evidence in favour of the former. Therefore, it appears that Bill Taube got it right: although red apples have nothing to do with ravens, it seems that his apple does indeed support the claim that all ravens are black.

This is highly counterintuitive, of course, and it is precisely why Hempel's puzzle is considered a paradox. In particular, it is very hard to believe that we learn something about ravens by observing apples. However, one solution to the paradox holds that this is exactly what occurs, it's just that in the case where there are a very large number of non-black objects, the amount that we learn is vanishingly small.

This argument becomes very complex in its detail, but it's possible to get a sense of how it works by imagining two different worlds: in the first, there are 2 ravens and a billion non-black objects; in the second, it's the other way around. If you observe a black raven in the first world, then this provides a lot of evidence in support of the claim that all ravens are black (since you have observed 50 per cent of all ravens). However, if you observe a single non-black object in this world, then, the evidence it provides in support of the claim that all ravens are black is vanishingly small, albeit non-zero.

In the second world, though, things are different. Here observing a single black raven provides very little evidence in support of the claim that all ravens are black (since there are as good as a billion other ravens, any one of which might not be black). However, in this world, observing a single non-black object, assuming it isn't a raven, provides a lot of evidence in support of the claim that all ravens are black, because there is only one other non-black object that could be a raven.

IS SMALL AND HAPPY BEST?

(see pages 16–17)

The idea that an overpopulated, dystopian country might be better than a much smaller country where everybody is happy is a version of an idea that was explored by the philosopher Derek Parfit in his book *Reasons and Persons*. He termed it the 'repugnant conclusion' (because it seems to be implied by utilitarianism) and formulated it as follows:

For any possible population of at least ten billion people, all with a very high quality of life, there must be some much larger imaginable population whose existence, if other things are equal, would be better even though its members have lives that are barely worth living.

The argument to show why this is the case has the following form. Imagine two countries, Country A, where everybody is happy, and Country A+, which is made up of two populations, the first which is identical to the population of Country A, and the second, an entirely separate population (perhaps separated from the country's other population by an ocean), which is much less happy, but where each person's life is still worth living. It is implausible to think that it would be better if this second, additional population did not exist. It doesn't affect the first population, and the lives of the people who comprise it still have value. It follows, then, that the situation in A+ is no worse than it is in A.

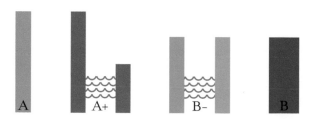

Now imagine a third country, B–, which also comprises two separate populations. This time the happiness of the second population has increased so it matches the happiness of the country's other population (whose happiness has decreased, but not by as much as the happiness of the second population has increased). It seems if anything Country B– must be better than Country A+, because there are greater levels of equality and the average level of happiness is higher.

Finally, there is Country B, which is identical to Country B–, except now the populations are no longer separated. It's hard to think that the lives of people in Country B are worse than those in Country B–, since the only thing that has changed is that the two populations have merged.

Mere Addition Paradox
This all adds up the the following: B is no worse than B–, which in turn no worse than A+ (and might be better than A+), and A+ is no worse than A. It follows, then, that Country B is no worse than Country A (and might even be better than Country A), even though it has a much larger population existing at a lower level of happiness.

This is counterintuitive enough, but consider that this series of steps can be repeated for Country B and then for a Country C, Country D and so on, until one reaches the repugnant conclusion that Country Z, which consists of a vast number of people whose lives are barely worth living, is no worse than Country A.

This argument is known as the 'mere addition paradox' and it's very hard to escape from without getting tied up in similarly perplexing complications. For example, perhaps you think that A+ is actually worse than A because the population has a lower average level of happiness. If so, this would certainly prevent the argument from establishing the repugnant conclusion. However, it would also seem to require thinking that a society consisting of ten incredibly happy people is preferable to a society of say one million slightly less, but still very happy people, despite the fact that total happiness would be vastly greater in the larger society.

It seems possible that Lindsey Rees could deploy her argument to persuade the Martians to spare her country. Perhaps there is something to the thought that if we think human life is intrinsically valuable then it's better if there's more of it (assuming we're talking about lives that are worth living). However, this is not a conclusion that Derek Parfit would accept. As far as he is concerned, the Repugnant Conclusion is precisely that — repugnant.

WHY DID THE BARBER FLEE TOWN?

(see pages 18–19)

The barber fled town because he didn't want to risk his life by violating Samson's new law, but couldn't figure out by whom he should be shaved.

The new town ordinance requires that every person keep themselves entirely bald by doing one or the other of two things (and not both):

1. Shaving themselves;

2. Visiting the barber to be shaved.

It follows from this that the barber shaves only those townsfolk who do not shave themselves. No problem, you might think, that sounds like a perfectly reasonable rule. Except it all gets a bit complicated when you begin to wonder about who shaves the barber.

The Barber Paradox

There are two possibilities here. Either he shaves himself or he is shaved by the barber (himself again). The trouble is both these possibilities end up violating Samson's new ordinance. If the barber shaves himself, then he is shaved by the barber, which is disallowed, so he mustn't shave himself. But if he doesn't shave himself, then he must shave himself, because every citizen who doesn't shave themselves is required to be shaved by the barber.

This conundrum is known as the Barber paradox, and is sometimes taken to be a version of Bertrand Russell's famous paradox, which asks whether the set of all sets that don't include themselves as members, should include itself as a member. Russell's paradox is genuinely paradoxical (if the set of all sets that don't include themselves as members doesn't include itself as a member, then it should, because it's a set that doesn't include itself as a member; but if it does include itself, then it shouldn't, because in that circumstance it's not a set that doesn't include itself as a member). However, this probably isn't the case with the Barber paradox, since the contradiction here is easy enough to escape by noting that a barber who both does and doesn't shave himself simply can't exist, which, of course, is precisely why our barber had to flee Zorah – there was no way he could uphold Samson's new ordinance.

There is a further variant of this puzzle that tends to crop up, which relies on a bit of verbal trickery for its solution. See if you can figure it out:

A barber from a small town makes the following claim: 'I shave all and only those men in our town who do not shave themselves'.

So who shaves the barber?

VALID OR INVALID?

(see pages 20–21)

Alex Gibbon is being asked here to assess the validity of three arguments. In this context, validity has a technical meaning: an argument is valid only if its conclusion is necessitated by its premises. The classic example of a valid argument is as follows:

All men are mortal. Socrates is a man. Therefore, Socrates is mortal.

Perhaps the most important thing to understand is that it is entirely possible for a valid argument to have conclusion that is not true. Consider:

All men have wings. Socrates is a man. Therefore, Socrates has wings.

This is a valid argument (the conclusion is necessitated by the premises), but its conclusion is false (because the first premise – All men have wings – is untrue). Now have a look at the arguments that Alex Gibbon has to assess.

Argument 1

Premise: All things that are smoked are good for the health
Premise: Cigarettes are smoked
Conclusion: Cigarettes are good for the health
This argument is valid. The conclusion is nonsense, of course, but it can be derived unequivocally from the premises.

Argument 2

Premise: All animals with four legs are dangerous
Premise: Poodles are not dangerous
Conclusion: Poodles are not animals with
four legs
This argument is also valid. If it
were true that all animals with four
legs are dangerous and also that

poodles are not dangerous, then it would necessarily follow that poodles are not animals with four legs. If this isn't clear, try substituting in different terms in the argument:

Premise: All humans are mortal

Premise: God is not mortal

Conclusion: God is not a human

Argument 3

Premise: All unemployed people are poor

Premise: Donald Trump is not unemployed

Conclusion: Donald Trump is not poor

This argument is not valid. Although the conclusion happens to be true, it doesn't follow from the premises because it's entirely possible that groups of people other than the unemployed are poor (the elderly, for example).

Belief Bias

These particular arguments are designed to illustrate a cognitive bias termed belief bias. Research conducted by psychologists such as Jonathan Evans shows that we're not particularly good at assessing the validity of deductive arguments when their conclusions are contrary to our beliefs. In other words, we have a tendency to reject valid arguments if their conclusions are unbelievable and accept invalid arguments if their conclusions are believable. This means if you've struggled with the arguments featured here, you can tell yourself this is not because you're generally bad at reasoning, it's because you're suffering from a cognitive bias.

WHAT WILL THE CROCODILE DO?

(see page 22)

The offer that The Crocodile has made Ronald Plump mimics what is known as The Crocodile Dilemma, which was first discussed by the ancient Greeks, and is sometimes attributed to the Stoic philosopher, Chrysippus: a crocodile promises to return a child he has stolen, if and only if, the father is able to tell him truly whether the crocodile will return the child or not.

If the father replies that the crocodile will return the child, then it is straightforward, with two possible outcomes:

1. The crocodile had determined to the return the child. The father has correctly identified what is going to happen, which means the crocodile will return his child as agreed.
2. The crocodile had determined not to return the child. The father has not correctly identified what is going to happen, which means the crocodile will keep his child (and presumably enjoy a nice snack).

Paradoxical Outcomes

However, things get tricky if the father replies that the crocodile will not return the child. Again there are two possible outcomes, but this time, both result in a paradox:

1. The crocodile had determined to return the child. The father has not correctly identified what is going to happen, which means the crocodile will keep his child. However, if the crocodile keeps his child, then it turns out the father has correctly identified what is going to happen, which means the crocodile should return his child.
2. The crocodile had determined not to return the child.

The father has correctly identified what's going to happen, which means the crocodile will return his child as agreed. However, if the crocodile returns his child, then it turns out the father has not correctly identified what is going to happen, which means the crocodile should keep his child.

These outcomes are paradoxical, since in neither case is it possible to determine whether the crocodile should return the child or not. This means the crocodile always has an excuse not to return the child, so if the father predicts that the crocodile will not return the child, he will never have a cast iron case that supports the return of his child.

So it is not entirely clear how Ronald Plump should respond to The Crocodile. He has two choices. He can either take a chance that The Crocodile's newly found conscience will have led him to decide to return his daughter, or, if he suspects that The Crocodile fully intends to secure a ransom payout, he can predict that The Crocodile will not return his daughter, and then hope to bamboozle him with the paradoxical consequence of such a prediction.

WHAT'S GOING ON WITH THE ANDROIDS?

(see pages 24–25)

The first stage in working out what's going on at El Santa is to realise that the only factor determining whether or not any particular android goes to the bar is a prediction about how many androids will turn up that evening. The androids know that if less than 60 of them turn up, then they will have a good time; if it's more than that, then they won't. This means the following rule is in play: an android goes to the bar if, and only if, she expects fewer than 60 to turn up, or stays at home if, and only if, she expects 60 or more to turn up.

Past Attendance

The next stage is to think about what sorts of factors might be relevant for a prediction about attendance, taking into account that the androids are unable to communicate with each other and must decide at exactly the same moment whether they are going to the bar. In the real world, factors such as the weather would be relevant, however, in his original treatment of this problem, economist W. Brian Arthur specified that the only thing that counts is the numbers who came in previous weeks.

This gives us a clue about what's going on. Suppose all the androids make their prediction about this week's attendance purely on the basis of last week's attendance. If fewer than 60 androids turned up last week, then fewer than 60 will turn up this week. If 60 or more androids turned up last week, then 60 or more will turn up this week.

The application of this rule would result in precisely the pattern of attendance that characterises Thursday night at the bar. Either all of the androids will turn up (because fewer than 60 of them turned up the previous week, so they all predict that fewer than 60 will turn up this week); or none of the androids will turn up (because 60 or more androids turned up last week, so they all predict that 60 or more will turn up this week).

The El Farol Bar Problem

However, no self-respecting android would make use of such a simple predictive rule and there is nothing to suggest that the only thing that can be factored into the prediction is the numbers who came in previous weeks. In fact, this doesn't make a difference. Regardless of the complexity of the predictive rule, if it is employed by all the androids and if it determines the prediction with a probability of one, then given the setup of what is now known as the El Farol bar problem, any android prediction will be self-defeating.

In other words, if they all predict that less than 60 will turn up, then in fact, they'll all turn up; and if they all predict that 60 or more of them will turn up, then in fact, none of them will turn up. This, of course, is precisely what has been happening. The androids have been programmed to utilise precisely the same predictive rule to determine whether or not to turn up at the bar and the consequence has been that they haven't yet got to enjoy their Kraftwerk theme night.

IS YOUR NEIGHBOUR A ZOMBIE?

(see pages 28–29)

Jorge is in a tough spot. He is confronted with a version of what philosophers have called the problem of other minds. Put simply, how we can be sure that (other) people have minds at all given that we don't have access to their internal mental states? The fact that people manifest behaviours doesn't seem to do it, since we can imagine sophisticated robots exhibiting the same behaviours without any kind of mentality. So perhaps Jorge is simply a biological automata.

Mental Worlds

Jorge can employ a number of arguments in his defence. The traditional response is the argument from analogy. This holds that it is possible to infer the existence of other minds from two facts:

A. All human beings have a similar physical makeup;
B. Other people behave in the same way I do in response to certain kinds of experiences.

Thus, if I stab myself with a knife, I will experience pain, and cry out. When other people stab themselves with knives, they too will cry out. Since we share the same physiology, it is reasonable to infer that they also experience pain.

This argument is plausible, but unfortunately for Jorge not decisive. The ghost hunters can simply object that it assumes what it is intended to

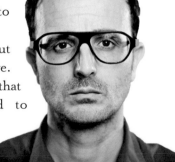

demonstrate: if you're physically identical to a properly functioning human being, then you have a mental world. The trouble is this doesn't seem to follow as a matter of logic: it is possible to imagine a world populated by biological automata – complicated machines that function as if they are human beings, but which have no awareness.

However, Jorge can respond that although there might be some possible world(s) in which human-like zombies are conceivable, in our world they are not, because of the existence of physical laws that link the physical properties of the brain to the existence of particular mental states. If this is right, then in our world possessing a functioning, human-like brain (even a sophisticated robot brain) is a guarantee of the existence of a mental world. If you've got brain state A, then you will experience pain B, no matter who or what you are.

A Way Out?

So is Jorge off the hook? Unfortunately, this argument doesn't quite settle the matter. It is possible simply to deny that brains together with the right physical laws are sufficient to generate consciousness. For example, one might be committed to the view that some kind of animating soul is also required for the existence of a mental world. If this is right, then the possibility of zombies is back in play. Although Jorge can construct a strong argument against the possibility of zombies, he cannot rule out them out beyond all possible doubt. He remains then in danger of evisceration.

Though, of course, it is possible that he simply won't care.

CAN YOU BE RESPONSIBLE
FOR WHAT IS UNAVOIDABLE?

(see pages 30-32)

It is a common thought that determinism — the view that every event is merely an effect of prior events and situations — undermines moral responsibility. The idea here is that it's not right to hold somebody responsible for what was always going to happen. If you can't make any choice other than the choice you actually make, then it seems it would be wrong to hold you responsible for that choice.

The thought experiment involving Goldtooth and Boris Huntington, which is based on a scenario originally developed by the philosopher Harry Frankfurt, is designed to challenge this line of thought. Huntington couldn't have made any choice other than to assassinate Bunny Amore because if he had, Goldtooth would have triggered the microchip, thereby ensuring Huntington went ahead with the assassination attempt. However, despite this fact, most people will likely think Huntington is morally responsible for killing Amore, since in fact the microchip was never needed. This seems to suggest it is possible to be morally responsible for a choice even if it's true that one could not have chosen otherwise.

The Truth of Determinism

However, as per usual, things are not as straightforward as they might at first appear. The difficulty here is that it is at least arguable that the scenario is question-begging: if determinism is true, then the microchip has nothing to do with why Boris Huntington was not able to act in any way other than he did act. Put simply, it follows from the truth of determinism that since the chip wasn't triggered, it was never going to be triggered and therefore it plays no part in this story. But if we take it out of the story and also make it clear that Boris Huntington couldn't have chosen other than to attempt to assissinate Bunny Amore (as is required by the truth of determinism), then likely people's intuitions will be very different about whether he was morally responsible for his act (that is, they will think that he was not).

The Falsity of Determinism

If, on the other hand, determinism is not true, then prior to assassinating Bunny Amore, Huntington must have made a series of choices that were not determined by prior events and situations. If so, then although he was always going to attempt to assassinate Bunny Amore (because of the microchip), it doesn't follow that he could not have originated a pattern of thoughts that in the absence of the chip would eventually have resulted in a decision not to assassinate Amore, and thus triggering the microchip. His moral responsibility then, assuming the falsity of determinism, lies in the fact that the microchip was not triggered, not in the fact that he ended up killing Bunny Amore; in other words, it lies in the fact that when he could have chosen another option, he did not.

IS TOM PEARCE TOM PEARCE?

(see page 32)

There is no generally agreed answer to the question of whether Tom Pearce will survive his trip to Lesser Bovey in the teletransporter. The issue at stake here has to do with personal identity and particularly the question of what is necessarily involved in the continued existence of a person over time.

If you believe that Tom will survive his trip, then likely you think that what counts for the survival of a person is some form of psychological continuity. To put it simply, you probably think a person will survive if they retain their memories, experiences and dispositions. If, on the other hand, you think that Tom will not survive his trip, then likely you think that bodily continuity is what counts. In other words, you probably think a person will survive so long as their body continues to exist in its currently integrated form. Although both of these views have their supporters, it is probably fair to say that most philosophers are attracted to some version of the psychological continuity idea.

Teleporter Malfunctions
However, to get an idea of the complexities involved in this debate, it is worth considering a variation on our story that was first suggested by the philosopher, Derek Parfit. In this variation, Tom gets into the teletransporter, presses the button, but nothing happens. He hears the whirring of the scanner, but he doesn't go anywhere. He steps out of the transporter and is informed that it has malfunctioned. The correct information about his body was passed on to the replicator in Bovey and his replica has been created (and is currently enjoying a cream tea at a local café), but his original

body wasn't destroyed, which is why it seems to him as if he hasn't gone anywhere. He's then given some bad news. He's been exposed to a fatal dose of radiation and he's not going to survive for more than a couple of days.

In this situation, should he be consoled by the thought that his replica lives on? If psychological continuity is what counts, then it seems that he has survived the trip, since his replica is psychologically continuous with the person he was before he stepped into the teletransporter. However, the problem here is precisely that it is hard to imagine being especially consoled by this thought (though one may think that it's better than nothing). Most people will think that the replica is not Tom Pearce, but merely somebody who thinks he's Tom Pearce. The real Tom Pearce didn't complete the trip, and is now looking at a vastly reduced lifespan.

WHAT'S MY POTENTIAL?

(see pages 34–35)

It is tempting to suppose that Moonchild always had the potential to father a child, but he was unlucky. The thought might be something to the effect that if he had made choice x, rather than choice y, then z would have occurred and he would have had a child. So the potential was there. In fact, it seems likely there were a large number of paths he could have followed that would have resulted in fatherhood, but he made wrong choices at crucial moments (i.e. to have sex with one woman rather than another).

Views of Determinism

However, it is not counterintuitive to suppose that the choices he made were choices that he was always going to make; in other words, he could not have acted in any way other than how he did. Certainly, this would be a standard view amongst people who believe determinism to be true – that every event, including human thought and behaviour, is necessitated by prior events and conditions. If determinism is true, it seems that Moonchild never had the potential to be a father; it's just there was no way of knowing this was true before the events transpired.

A possible response here would be to claim that what we know about the laws of physics and particularly quantum mechanics, rules out determinism. To put it simply, there is enough randomness in nature to mean it doesn't follow that because conditions x prevail at time y, outcome z is inevitable. If outcome z isn't inevitable — if it isn't inevitable that Monchild won't have children — then it follows that it might still make sense to talk in terms of people having potentials that don't come to pass.

The Concept of Potential

Unfortunately, this argument isn't decisive. Partly because it isn't clear that quantum indeterminacy functions at the level of human acts and choices, but also because even if it does, it may not be enough to rescue the concept of potential.

Suppose, you want to be the world's fastest sprinter. Presumably, this isn't any sort of real possibility (many apologies if it so happens you're Usain Bolt). But then one day some random event occurs and triggers a chain reaction that results in you getting struck by lightning. As a result, you can now run 100 metres in eight seconds. The question is: do we really want to say that you had the potential to run 100m in eight seconds all along?

It is important to recognise that we're not talking about the absence of free will here (since many philosophers believe that free will is compatible with determinism). We're discussing whether it makes sense to think there is such a thing as 'potential that will never be fulfilled'. If determinism is true, then it is hard to see how this can be the case and if it isn't the case, it means there never were going to be baby Moonchilds cluttering up the world.

WHO GETS TORTURED?

(see pages 36–37)

This scenario normally elicits the response that Kassandra should choose Body-Person A - that is, the person whose body previously belonged to her, but who now has Susannah's thoughts, memories and dispositions - as the person to be tortured. This suggests that most people think personal identity is primarily a matter of psychological continuity or connectedness. In other words, they think personal identity follows the mind, not the body.

However, the philosopher, Bernard Williams, has pointed out that it is possible to present this scenario in a different way in order to elicit the opposite conclusion.

Separating the Self

Suppose that somebody tells you that you're going to be tortured tomorrow morning, but then adds that when the time comes, you won't remember anything you now remember. Likely you won't be consoled by this thought, since it's possible to imagine losing one's memory after an accident, for example, and yet still experiencing great pain.

You're then informed that at the moment of torture not only will you not have your current memories, you'll actually have the memories of somebody else. Again it seems as if you would not be reassured by this thought, since it is possible

to imagine being in a delirious state, and thinking that one is Henry VIII, for example, and yet still suffering horribly under torture.

It also seems unlikely you'll be reassured by the further revelation that when the time comes you'll actually have the memories of a person who is living right now, and that they'll have been implanted into your brain, since it doesn't seem to make much difference whose memories in particular you will have, or how they came to be in your mind. If you weren't reassured before, there's no reason why you'd be reassured now.

The key point here is that this series of events exactly describes one side of what Kassandra and Susannah are about to go through, and yet the intuition is entirely different. Now it seems that what is going to happen to the body is what is crucial. If it were not, then we would not remain fearful of torture. According to Bernard Williams, this makes the whole situation 'totally mysterious':

> When we look at these two differences of presentation, can we really convince ourselves that the second presentation is wrong or misleading, thus leaving the road open to the first version which at the time seemed so convincing? Surely not.

It is clear then that the way we present these kinds of scenarios can make a vast difference to the intuitions they elicit.

WHAT IF MONTY DOESN'T KNOW?

(see pages 40–41)

This variant of the Monty Hall problem is known as 'Ignorant Monty' or 'Monty Fall'. The set-up is identical to the original Monty Hall problem, except in this version Monty either doesn't know what lies behind the doors (and happens to open one that doesn't reveal the car); or, as in this case, he opens a door at random, which happens not to reveal the car.

The temptation is to think that because the set-up is identical to the original version and in neither case does Monty reveal the car, the probability of winning if you choose to switch must be the same in both cases. This is wrong. The probability of winning if you switch in the original version is two-thirds. In this variant, there is no benefit to switching: the probability of winning is 50:50 whether you switch or not. Therefore, there is no particular reason for William to switch doors here. Although he won't harm his chances by doing so, he's not going to improve them either.

It's possible you're a little baffled by all this. How can two scenarios be seemingly identical, yet given the same strategy — i.e. switching — the probability of winning is different in each case?

The Probabilities
The first thing to do is to show that the probability of winning is 50:50 whether you switch or not in this new variant of the problem. Let's start by assuming

you select Door 1 and Monty then randomly opens Door 3. The next step is to work out what the probability is that Door 3 does not contain the car in all possible situations (i.e. if the car is behind Door 1, Door 2 and Door 3 respectively).

This is easy enough: if the car is behind either Door 1 or Door 2, then in both cases the probability that Door 3 does not contain the car is one (i.e. it is certain it doesn't contain the car, because in both cases the car is behind a different door); if the car is behind Door 3, then the probability that Door 3 does not contain the car is zero (i.e. there is no chance it doesn't contain the car, because it does contain the car).

Therefore, as Door 3 does not contain the car (because Monty revealed a goat when he fell against it), it follows that the car must be behind either Door 1 or 2. We also know the probability that Door 3 does not contain the car is no more likely if the car is behind Door 1 than it is if it is behind Door

THE CAR IS BEHIND	PROBABILITY THAT DOOR 3 DOES NOT CONTAIN THE CAR
Door 1	1
Door 2	1
Door 3	0

2. It follows, therefore, that there is a 50:50 chance that the car is behind either of these doors and there is nobenefit to switching.

Understanding the Variant

The key to understanding the difference between the original Monty Hall problem and this variant is to appreciate that the host is sometimes inadvertently going to reveal the car (because his 'choice' of the door is random), thereby ending the game before it has started. This is significant because given the original Monty Hall scenario and the exact same situation – assuming you had chosen the same door, and the goats and Ferrari were in the same place – on each of these occasions, you would have ended up winning the car had you switched (because to avoid revealing the Ferrari, Monty would have been forced to reveal the other goat, meaning had you switched, you would have switched to the door with the car). It is this difference that explains why the probability of winning if you switch is two-thirds given the original Monty Hall scenario and only 50:50 in the variant. To put it simply, there are occasions where you can't win in the Monty Fall variant, where you would have won given the original Monty Hall set-up.

SHOULD YOU RUN OVER THE FAT MAN?

(see pages 42–43)

The 'Trolley Problem', which was first described by the philosopher, Philippa Foot, has the following standard form:

A trolley is running out of control down a track. In its path are five people who have been tied to the track. Fortunately, you can hit a button, which will send the trolley down a different track to safety. Unfortunately, there is a single person tied to that track. Should you hit the button or do nothing?

Most people respond that the trolley should be diverted, which suggests we have a strong intuition that where there is no choice it is sometimes justified to act in a way that has the effect of harming some number of people if it means that a greater number of people are spared harm.

The scenario featured in this book is the 'loop back' variation of the Trolley Problem. The set up is identical, except in this case the train is diverted onto a track that loops back around so that if it weren't for the presence of the single, fat man on the track, the trolley would still kill the five people. The significance of this variation can only properly be understood by first considering another version of the Trolley Problem.

The Fat Man and the Railway Bridge

The philosopher, Judith Jarvis Thomson, posed the following variation of the Trolley Problem:

A trolley is running out of control down a track towards five people. You are on a bridge under which it will pass, and you can stop it by dropping a heavy weight in front of it. As it happens, there is a very fat man next to you – your only way to stop the trolley is to push him over the bridge and onto the track, killing him to save five. Should you push the fat man onto the track?

The moral calculation here seems to be the same as it was in the original version of the problem. You can sacrifice the life of one person – the fat man – in order to save the lives of five other people. However, we tend to have very different intuitions about the fat man scenario: most people think it would be wrong to push the him off the bridge.

The Doctrine of Double Effect

So why do we have these different intuitions? A possible explanation is that there is a genuine moral difference between the two scenarios. In the original Trolley Problem, we can save the five people on the track without intending to do any harm to the single person tied to the other track: our intention is simply to divert the train away from the five people it is running towards. This is permissible under what is termed the doctrine of double effect, which asserts (amongst other things) that so long as we don't intend a bad effect, even as a means to a good effect, then an action is justified if the good effect sufficiently outweighs the bad effect. Significantly, it is clear that pushing the fat man off the bridge doesn't pass this test: here we're specifically using the fat man in order to achieve the good effect (i.e., saving the five people).

However, the idea that the difference in our intuitions about these two scenarios has to do with whether we're using somebody as a means to an end is thrown into doubt by the loop back variation of the Trolley Problem. In this variation, the success of our plan depends on the presence of the fat man on the track. If he isn't there, the five people die anyway. It's only by running him down that we get to save them. So, just as in the case of the fat man on the bridge, this is ruled out by the doctrine of double effect. However, when presented with the loop back variation, and unlike in the case of the fat man on the bridge, people tend to reply that diverting the trolley (train) is morally justified.

If you're feeling perplexed by all this, then it might be a comfort to know that there isn't really a right answer here. The importance of the Trolley Problem, and its variants, is precisely that it shows that the reasons for our moral intuitions are not always obvious.

IS ZEUS LOSING HIS POWER?

The puzzle that Zeus is wrestling with here is known as the paradox of omnipotence. The Australian philosopher, J. L. Mackie, specified the problem as follows:

> *[C]an an omnipotent being make things which he cannot subsequently control? Or ... can an omnipotent being make rules which then bind himself? [...] It is clear that this is a paradox: the questions cannot be satisfactorily answer either in the affirmative or in the negative. If we answer 'Yes', it follows that if God actually makes things which he cannot control, or makes rules which bind himself, he is not omnipotent once he has made them: there are then things which he cannot do. But if we answer 'No', we are immediately asserting that there are things which he cannot do, that is to say he is already not omnipotent.*

However, Mackie is much too quick to declare this puzzle a genuine paradox, because there are a number of escape routes available to Zeus — and other omnipotent gods (in other possible worlds) — if he wants to hold on to his claim that he is omnipotent.

The first holds that omnipotence requires only the power to bring about states of affairs that are logically possible. Thus, for example, Aquinas argues that to think that omnipotence requires the ability to bring about absolutely any state of affairs, including impossible states of affairs, is to assert a contradiction, since it requires the impossible to be possible. In this sense, then, Mackie sets the bar too high in supposing that an omnipotent being must have the power to make things that he subsequently cannot control, since this requires the ability to do what is ruled out as a matter of logic, and it is not a limit on the power of an omnipotent being that it cannot do the impossible.

However, though the overwhelming consensus amongst philosophers is that omnipotence does not require the ability to do the impossible, there are dissenting voices. Rene Descartes, for example, argued that:

> [W]e can be quite certain that God can do whatever we are able to understand, but not that He cannot do what we are unable to understand. For it would be presumptuous to think that our imagination extends as far as His power.

Of course, if omnipotence does require the ability to do the impossible, then the paradox of omnipotence emerges again, and it seems that Zeus's godly prowess is once more under threat. However, he has little to fear, because of the following thought. If an omnipotent being can do absolutely anything, then this would include the ability to rewrite the rules of logic in a way that mere humans cannot begin to comprehend. Therefore, it follows that if Zeus is omnipotent in this sense, he could create a mountain he cannot move, and yet at the same time be able to move it. To us, this seems straightforwardly contradictory, but that's a comment on our limitations, rather than Zeus's.

IS IT NECESSARILY WRONG TO EAT PEOPLE?

(see pages 46–47)

This tale is a version of a scenario set out in a famous article by Lon L. Fuller called 'The Case of the Speluncean Explorers', published in the *Harvard Law Review* in 1949. The issues it raises are complex and subtle, and a voluminous literature has built up around them. Consequently, it is not possible to give a definitive answer to the question of whether the Cradock Four should be convicted of murder. However, it is possible to get a sense of the sorts of arguments that are relevant here.

Law of the Land

The first point to make is that one must not assume that what is key is whether the Cradock Four did something morally wrong. It is entirely possible to think that the issue of morality has no bearing on whether the group is guilty of the crime of murder. This is the view of 'Justice Keen', one of the characters in Fuller's original article:

> *[A] question that I wish to put to one side is that of deciding whether what these men did was 'right' or 'wrong,' 'wicked' or 'good.' That is ... irrelevant to the discharge of my office as a judge sworn to apply, not my conceptions of morality, but the law of the land.*

In our scenario, the law of the land is clear. If a person wilfully takes the life of another then they will be punished by death. Although this appears to support the view that the Cradock Four should be executed for their crimes, there are a number of ways that one can chip away at this conclusion.

For instance, one might argue that the law simply doesn't apply in a situation such as the one faced by the Cradock Four.

In Fuller's article, 'Justice Foster' argues that the enacted law of a country only applies where it remains possible for a people to coexist peacefully. This was not the case for the group trapped in the cavern. The continued survival of any of them depended upon them taking the life of one of their number. In effect, a kind of 'law of nature' held sway that was derived from principles that were appropriate to their particular situation. In these terms, the Cradock Four must be seen as being 'guiltless of any crime'.

A Matter of Interpretation

A second possibility relies on a distinction between the letter of the law and the law itself. If the law is not designed to be interpreted literally, then perhaps the fact that the Cradock Four broke the letter of the law does not entail that they are guilty of the crime of murder. Consider, for example, the excuse of self-defence. In English law, the right to self-defence allows a person to act in a way that would otherwise be illegal if they have good reason to believe that they are under imminent threat. Obviously, the Cradock Four could not claim self-defence, but it is possible they could argue that the existence of the excuse of self-defence shows that it is not the letter of the law that is crucial in these sorts of outlier cases.

Public Opinion

There is also the thought that there needs to be flexibility in how the law is applied in order for the legal system to retain the confidence of a country's citizens. If a trial produces a result that is wildly out of kilter with public opinion, then the accord between judiciary, legal process and citizenry is threatened. Therefore, in a case such as this one, there is an argument for seeking out past precedents that would justify the freeing of the perpetrators. 'Justice Hardy' expresses this point as follows:

> *Declaring these men innocent need not involve us in any undignified quibble or trick. No principle of statutory construction is required that is not consistent with the past practices of this Court. Certainly no layman would think that in letting these men off we had stretched the statute any more than our ancestors did when they created the excuse of self-defense.*

These arguments are not decisive, of course. The result of the (fictional) deliberations reported in Fuller's article was that the sentence of death should stand. This was also the verdict in the Mignonette Case, a nineteenth century real-life analog of our fictional scenario (albeit the death sentence in this instance was later commuted). Nevertheless, the continuing interest in these sorts of cases is testament to the difficulty of the issues at stake.

WHAT WILL HAPPEN AT THE ROBBER'S CAVE?

(see pages 50–51)

Bill Silverman is absolutely right to be worried about what is going to unfold at this year's Robber's Cave scout camp. In a sense, this is just a matter of common sense. We know from experience that hostility between social groups is integrally bound up with conflicts of interest. In other words, there is nothing particularly contentious in the thought that groups often fall into conflict because they are in various ways in competition with each other. There is also evidence to support this proposition from one of the most famous field experiments ever conducted in the history of social psychology: the Robber's Cave Experiment.

The Robber's Cave Experiment

Muzafer Sherif and his colleagues wanted to find out whether competition between groups was a sufficient condition for the emergence of hostility.

> *Our working hypothesis was that when two groups have conflicting aims — i.e., when one can achieve its ends only at the expense of the other — their members will become hostile to each other even though the groups are composed of normal well-adjusted individuals.*

The experiment was conducted in 1954 at a summer camp in Oklahoma, near a Jesse James hideaway called Robber's Cave. Twenty-two boys, all 'healthy, socially well-adjusted, somewhat above average in intelligence, and from stable, white, Protestant, middle-class homes', were split into two groups, which were then kept apart to allow separate group identities to emerge. The experimenters facilitated this

process by organising a number of cooperative activities for each group, including cooking, organised games and tent pitching. The two groups, whose members began to refer to themselves as the Rattlers and Eagles, very quickly developed group norms, hierarchies and a significant esprit de corps.

After about a week, the Rattlers and Eagles were introduced to each other, and a potential source of conflict was added into the mix. Just as in our scenario, the experimenters announced the two groups were to compete against each other in a series of organised games — baseball, tug-of-war, a treasure hunt, and the like — after which one group would be declared the overall winner.

Although at first the boys made some concessions to sportsmanship, the contests very rapidly degenerated into something akin to a Lord of the Flies reenactment. The Rattlers and the Eagles burned each other's flags, they fought, exchanged insults, sent raiding parties to each other's living quarters, stole from one another, and were generally at each other's throats.

The Outcome
Sherif and his colleagues described the outcome thus:

As a consequence of repeated interaction between the two experimentally formed groups in competitive and reciprocally frustrating

situations, and of the cumulative intergroup friction thus engendered, negative attitudes toward the out-group were formed by members of each in-group. These negative attitudes toward the out-group, crystallized in unfavorable stereotypes, were manifested by name-calling, derogation of the out-group, and the explicit desire to avoid association with the out-group...

The Robber's Cave Experiment then provides evidence for the proposition that antagonism and hostility between social groups is linked to conflicts of interest.

But this is not quite the end of the story. You will have noticed that in our scenario if the boys already knew each other then the competition between the two groups was claimed to have passed off without incident. Although this runs contrary to the view of Sherif and his colleagues that intergroup conflict is a sufficient condition for the emergence of hostility, there is some evidence to support our version of things. In particular, a study of English boy scouts by Tyerman and Spencer in 1983 found precisely that in a situation where there are preexisting friendship ties, competition between groups remains friendly, and there is no increase in in-group solidarity at the expense of the out-group, or in inter-group conflict.

IS HOMO SAPIENS A NOBLE SAVAGE?

(see page 52)

Unfortunately for Alex Gibbon's utopian dreams, evidence suggests that the distinction between Us and Them is foundational in shaping and structuring human experience. Almost certainly then this means we're going to have to get used to living in a world characterised by radical schisms between people and groups.

Consider the work of psychologist Henri Tajfel and his colleagues in the 1970s. In their experiments, a person was given a trivial task to complete — for example, guessing the number of dots in a cluster — and then assigned to an individual cubicle and told that his job was to allocate points to two other people that could be exchanged for money after the experiment. He was then informed that he had been allocated a particular 'group' on the basis of whether he underestimated or overestimated the number of dots in the cluster. He was also told about the group membership of the two people to whom he had to allocate points/money.

The idea was to determine whether this kind of minimal group membership would be a factor in the way that people distributed awards; in other words, would people tend to discriminate in favour of people in their own group.

The results were startling. People were quite willing to discriminate in favour of the person who shared their group. Even when offered a choice, people sought to maximise the difference between what was awarded to the in-group member and what was awarded to the out-group member, even if this meant that the in-group person received less overall than via an alternative strategy. In other words, what was crucial was how well the in-group member did relative to the out-group.

It is important to be clear about what was going on here. The people involved: (a) didn't know each other; (b) had not interacted with each other; (c) were under no explicit pressure to favour their own group; and (d) stood to gain nothing personally by favouring their own group. Yet despite this, people were willing to discriminate against a person they knew nothing about just because they had been allocated to a different group.

This suggests that we inevitably see ourselves in terms of our membership of specific social groups and that we structure our understanding of the world in terms of distinctions between in-groups and out-groups. Henri Tajfel puts this point as follows:

> *In our judgements of other people, in forming stereotypes, in learning a second language, in our work relations, we do not act as isolated individuals, but as social beings who derive an important part of our identity from the human groups and social categories we belong to; and we act in accordance with this awareness.*

For as long as this is the case, then it is overwhelmingly likely that conflict and opposing groups will remain, and Alex Gibbon's utopian dream will remain just that.

WILL HELP ARRIVE?

(see pages 54–55)

The event that Goldilocks vaguely recalls learning about is the slaying of a young woman called Kitty Genovese in New York City in 1964. The incident was witnessed by 38 different people, yet not one of them called the police during the 30-minute attack.

The Bystander Effect

Exactly why bystanders tend to avoid becoming involved in this sort of emergency situation has been extensively studied by social psychologists. The picture is complicated, of course, but a 'bystander effect' has been identified, which predicts that the more people who witness an event, the less likely it is that any particular person will become involved.

Partly, this has to do with conformity. People tend to take their cue from the inactivity of their fellow witnesses, reasoning that if the situation warranted action, then somebody else would already have become involved. It is a dilution of responsibility; knowing you're not alone in witnessing an emergency allows you to tell yourself that you have no particular responsibility to become involved. Thus, in the Kitty Genovese case, it seems likely that each witness assumed that somebody else would call the police.

This all paints a rather depressing picture – we look for excuses to avoid helping others. However, in the particular situation faced by Goldilocks, there is room for optimism.

The Mutuality Factor

The social psychologist, Elliot Aronson, relates the story of how he once heard somebody cry out while he was camping in

Yosemite National Park. He crawled out of his tent, only to be confronted by something he took to be very strange.

> From all over the area, myriad flickering lights were converging on a single point. These were lanterns and flashlights being carried by dozens of campers running to the aid of the individual who had screamed. It turned out that his scream had been one of surprise caused by a relatively harmless flare-up in his gasoline stove. The other campers seemed almost disappointed when no help was needed.

Aronson suggests that people had been willing to become involved in this situation because of a feeling of 'mutuality', engendered by their common circumstances. In other words, even though the campers didn't know each other, they felt a common bond, which meant they were predisposed to come to each other's aid in the event of trouble.

This supposition is borne out by a subsequent experiment conducted by Irving Piliavin and his colleagues. They found that if a person 'collapsed' on a New York subway train, then almost always people would rush to help. It appears that merely sharing a train carriage is enough to convince passengers that somehow they share a common fate, which in turn predisposes them towards helping behaviour.

Therefore, there is a good chance that Goldilocks' fellow campers will come to her aid if she calls for help. This is not because human beings are especially inclined to help each other out — we're not — but because in this particular situation, her fellow campers will likely feel a common bond with her because they share similar circumstances.

WHOM DO YOU PREFER?

(see pages 56–57)

Peter Campbell is right to predict that Group A will judge Zach Coine more positively than Group B. This is somewhat surprising given that the words are identical in both groups: intelligent, industrious, impulsive, critical, stubborn, envious. As you probably noticed, the only difference is the order of the words. In the case of Group A, the positive traits appeared first; for Group B, it was the other way around. The interesting thing is that this switch makes all the difference in terms of how we perceive the person being described.

We know this to be the case because of a groundbreaking piece of research undertaken in 1946 by the social psychologist, Soloman Asch, who conducted precisely the experiment Peter Campbell was required to observe. He found that Group A saw the person in a largely positive way: he is able, has shortcomings, but these do not overshadow his good qualities. Group B, in contrast, saw the person as being a 'problem', whose merits were significantly undermined by his flaws. Moreover, some of the qualities that were interpreted positively by Group A (such as impulsiveness) were interpreted negatively by Group B.

The Primary Effect

This result suggests that what we learn first about something can have a disproportionate effect on how we perceive it. This has been termed the 'primacy effect' and it is contrasted with the 'recency effect' (which describes the greater impact of what we learn later on). A number of explanations have been offered for the existence of a primacy effect. For example, it is possible that we assume what is first revealed is 'real', and then discount anything that later on runs counter to it; or that we simply pay more attention to what we learn early on; or that we interpret everything we learn later on through the 'filter' of what we learned first (so, for example, if we decide early on that a person is intelligent, we'll interpret their other qualities — even qualities that could be seen as being negative — in terms of this original assessment).

There are a number of rather disturbing implications of the existence of a primacy effect (and indeed of its opposite, the recency effect). Perhaps most significantly it suggests that our ability to form judgements about something is subject to a systematic bias: the order in which information is presented makes a difference to the judgements we form that is not justified by the information itself.

Consider, for example, the following scenario. You are interviewing two candidates for a job. Both are given verbal examinations, and they get an identical number of questions right in the exam. However, Candidate A performs better in the early part of the exam; Candidate B in the latter part of the exam. In this situation, you are likely to judge Candidate A as the more competent even though this is not justified by their overall performance. Your ability to make an accurate assessment will likely be been undermined by the cognitive bias that constitutes the primacy effect.

HOW ABOUT A DATE?

(see pages 58-59)

Jerry Chow is undoubtedly right to think that there are advantages to being physically attractive. Consider, for example, the following study by Karen Dion and her colleagues. They showed college students photographs of three people of differing levels of attractiveness – one attractive, one average and one unattractive – and then asked the students to rank the people in the pictures across a series of personality traits and also to predict their future happiness. The physically attractive person was overwhelmingly judged to have the most positive traits and the best chance of future happiness. In light of this result, it is perhaps no surprise that in another piece of research, Chris Downs and Philip Lyons found that judges tend to levy a higher fine when dealing with an unattractive person guilty of a misdemeanour than when dealing with a similarly guilty attractive person.

Skin Deep
Although there is a lot of research that shows the same kind of thing, it is still hard to imagine that physical attractiveness is so important when it comes to romantic entanglements. Not least, we like to suppose that we are too sophisticated to judge people solely in terms of their appearance, which, after all, is something over which we have little control. Unfortunately, our sophistication goes just about as skin-deep as our beauty, because the evidence overwhelmingly suggests that attractiveness is an important determinant of liking and loving.

In a classic study, conducted at the University of Minnesota in 1966, Elaine Walster and her colleagues randomly matched up first-year students for a dance date. The students had previously completed a set of tests that provided information about their personality, intelligence, social skills, and the like. In addition, they were ranked for physical attractiveness. The question was which factors were most important in determining whether a couple liked each other. It was not, as one might suppose from a quick perusal of a lonely hearts column, intelligence or a sense of humour. In fact, attractiveness was the only significant determinant of whether a couple wanted to meet again. If two attractive people were paired with each other, then they were most likely to arrange a second date.

The view espoused by Jerry's mother that attractiveness is more than skin deep is very popular. If you ask people what they want in a potential partner, for example, then attractiveness tends to come a long way down the list. However, the evidence tells us something different: physical attractiveness is in fact right at the centre of the story of liking and loving.

HOW OBEDIENT ARE WE?

(see page 60)

David Jared is correct to believe that in the sorts of circumstances he described (notwithstanding the brain transplant aspect) most people would be willing to torture another human being. This rather shocking fact was first demonstrated in a series of classic experiments conducted by the psychologist, Stanley Milgram, in the early 1960s.

The Remote-Victim Experiment

The first of Milgram's experiments, now known as the remote-victim experiment, featured 40 male participants, who had each responded to a newspaper advert for a study supposedly looking at the effects of punishment on learning. They were allocated to a 'teacher' role and then paired with an experimenter's stooge, who would play the 'learner'. Everything that subsequently happened was scripted, except, of course, for the actions and reactions of each participant.

The learner was strapped into a chair and attached to electrodes. The experimenter and teacher then moved to an adjoining room where a shock generator was located, which administered an electric shock every time the learner made an error. The teacher was given a small electric shock to convince him that the set-up was real (which, of course, it wasn't).

The teacher then gave a memory test and each time the learner made a mistake, he delivered an electric shock, increasing the intensity by 15 volts for each mistake.

The stunning result of this experiment was that every teacher was willing to deliver a shock up to 300 volts, which was labelled 'intense shock' on the machine and which caused the learner to pound desperately on the wall. Moreover, nearly two-thirds of participants were willing to give the highest possible shock of 450 volts, despite the fact the learner appeared to be non-responsive by this point. This level of shock was marked 'XXX' on the machine, one stage beyond the level labelled 'danger: severe shock'.

These results were not confined to this one experiment; Milgram found a similar pattern of responses across a total of 18 different experiments, incorporating the responses of 646 participants (including 40 women, who also showed a 65 per cent obedience rate). This led Milgram to conclude that, 'ordinary people simply doing their jobs without any particular hostility on their part, can become agents in a terrible destructive process.'

Although the results of Milgram's experiments are by now well-known, most people still claim that they would not obey in this situation. Social psychologist, Elliot Aronson, asks his new intake of students every year if they would be willing to inflict severe pain on another person in a similar situation and each time, 99 per cent say no. However, as we have seen, the evidence suggests otherwise.

Although none of this lets David Jared off the hook, it does suggest that there is nothing particularly exceptional about his behaviour. We like to think that we are immune to situational pressures, but the reality is that most people can probably be induced to do terrible things given the right circumstances.

WHO SHOULD LIZZY CHOOSE?
(see pages 62-64)

It is likely you think that the idea that relationships can be reduced to calculations about relative rewards (such as attractiveness and intelligence) is absurd.

However, the strategy of analysing liking and loving in terms of a market exchange of rewards and costs is generally fruitful. The key proposition is that we like people whose behaviour brings maximum rewards at minimum costs. It is this that explains why we like people who behave nicely more than we like those who do not, and people who share our views more than those who do not.

The Matching Hypothesis

This idea has led researchers to hypothesise that similarity of attractiveness will be a crucial factor in determining whether or not a relationship is long-lasting. The idea is that we expect our relationships to be more or less equal in terms of their rewards and costs, and attractiveness is considered a reward. Therefore, we seek out people who reward us at roughly the same level as we reward them.

The evidence in favour of this 'matching hypothesis' is persuasive. It shows that people in committed relationships tend to be more similar in physical attractiveness than one would expect to occur by chance. Bernard Murstein, for example, in a study of 99 established couples found significantly less discrepancy in their attractiveness than in the attractiveness of artificially paired couples.

However, one must be careful not to oversimplify the market exchange aspects of liking and loving. It is true that we tend to like people who offer rewards at little cost. But, as

Elliot Aronson points out in his classic text, *The Social Animal*, what counts as a reward in any specific situation is hard to judge. Thus, Aronson notes that while we like to be praised and tend to like the person who praises, we don't like it so much if the praise is too fulsome, or unwarranted, or if it appears to be self-serving.

Nevertheless, it remains true that from a psychological point of view, there is little that is intractably mysterious about liking and loving. We form relationships with people because we find them in various ways rewarding. There is complexity in the detail, but the principle is straightforward enough.

None of this means that Lizzy Bennett should necessarily choose William as her partner for a romantic getaway. However, her intuition that there is an exchange dimension to relationships is spot on. If she chooses Charlie, and it turns out that he is much more attractive than she is, then evidence suggests that any relationship that develops will have less chance of success than it would have done had they both been of similar levels of attractiveness.

IS IT RATIONAL TO BELIEVE IN MONSTERS UNDER THE BED?

(see pages 64-65)

The issue we're dealing with here is whether it is reasonable to assert the truth of a belief purely on the basis of an experience that apparently confirms the belief. This might not be thought to be reasonable. We know that people can be fooled by their experiences, for example, we know that people hallucinate and that often they cannot tell the difference between the hallucination and reality.

Believing What You See

The challenge of this thought experiment is that it asks us to imagine a situation where it does seem reasonable to believe that something is real even though one recognises that the experience might be misleading. Consider, for example, how you would react if you were in Boris's shoes and somebody told you that you were being unreasonable in fleeing the monster. Likely you wouldn't be impressed. The experience of the monster is veridical; the stakes are unimaginably high — the monster is right there in your face and about to attack and monsters are not ruled out as a matter of logic. Therefore, even if you recognise you might be hallucinating, you're probably not going to think it is unreasonable to believe you are not. Moreover, it's not going to seem unreasonable on calm reflection afterwards.

The claim here then is that if a belief is not ruled out as a matter of logic, and if it is of utmost and immediate personal significance, it can be reasonable to assert or accept its truth purely on the basis of its being confirmed by your own veridical (seeming beyond doubt) experience.

A Matter Of Faith

If this is right, then part of what is interesting is that it might justify certain sorts of religious belief. Consider, for example, that many religious believers claim both that their experience of the divine is veridical and also that belief in the truth of the experience can be a matter of life or death importance.

This second point is easily enough understood: think, for instance, about the mother who has lost a child, and yearns to be reunited with her in the afterlife; or the soldier in the First World War struggling against the temptation to desert in the knowledge that he has to go over the trenches in the morning; or simply the sceptical believer who in experiencing what seems to be the divine is profoundly unnerved by the idea that if the experience is true then it's possible he'll lose everything if he does not accept its truth.

There are complications here, of course. Not least, one could argue endlessly about what exactly 'reasonable' means in this context. However, even if one does not accept that it is reasonable for Boris to believe that the monster exists, it is certainly understandable if he does, and even this can function as a justification (of sorts) for religious belief.

WHEN IS A BELIEF NOT A BELIEF?
(see pages 66-67)

The first thing to say here is that there isn't necessarily a right answer to either of these questions. This is partly because it isn't entirely clear that it is psychologically possible for human beings to be blissfully happy for eternity. Indeed, it is a common thought that living forever would actually turn out to be something of a nightmare. A possible response here is to claim that eternity would be a transformative experience, so much so that it does make sense to think that two people could be blissfully happy together for the rest of time. However, this response raises a whole set of different problems to do with the nature of personal identity. In particular, it isn't clear that a person so transformed that they were able to endure eternity without descending into madness would be the same person as they were when mortal.

Eternal Life
Nevertheless, despite all this, the story of David and Nicola, and the possibility of their endless love, remains interesting because people certainly claim to believe in eternal life, and that it will be blissful and spent with loved ones. However, claiming to believe something, and actually believing it, are two different things, so a relevant question is whether we should take claims of such a belief at face-value. In other words, should we take people at their word when they tell us they believe in everlasting life? It is this issue that the story of David and Nicola is designed to shed light upon.

The are various points to make in this regard. The first is that if it's true that David and Nicola genuinely believe they can choose to be blissfully happy together forever, and that this is what they want, then surely one would expect them to make this choice, even if it meant they would have to spend the next twenty years apart. After all, twenty years separation is a tiny price to pay for an eternity of happiness together: it represents an infinitesimally small interlude in their relationship.

Perhaps more significantly, though, one would also expect their misery at being parted to be significantly mitigated by the certainty they'll see each other again and that when they do everything will be wonderful. It is true, of course, that they are bound to experience twenty years as being a long time, so in that sense we would expect them to grieve for the absence of each other, but even so we're not talking here about a situation where they'll never see each other again, or, even a situation where they'll be reunited but subject to the usual vicissitudes of everyday life, we're talking about them being reunited in a state of everlasting bliss — where their lives will be everything they could possibly hope for. So, by all means, one would expect them to grieve, but not to fall into despair.

The Afterlife
The final point to make here is that anybody who believes in life after death, and that it will be spent in blissful togetherness with loved ones, is in a situation closely analogous to that of David and Nicola when it comes to facing up to their own mortality and that of their loved ones. And yet many such

people do fall into despair when their husband or wife or child dies; they do cling desperately onto life, as if this life is the only life they will live; and they do not look forward to the prospect of dying even though they claim to believe that death is the gateway to a better future.

There is a common idea that there are no atheists in foxholes: in the face of extreme danger, even non-believers tend to offer up a prayer to some kind of deity. However, as the philosopher Julian Baggini points out, it also seems there are no theists at funerals. Certainly, the way in which the overwhelming majority of people react to the death of a loved one does not sit easily with the idea that all that has occurred is a temporary hiatus in a relationship that will actually endure forever.

ARE WE BRAINS IN VATS?

(see page 70)

The brain in a vat thought experiment, which was popularised in the *Matrix* films, is designed to challenge the proposition that we can ever have certain knowledge of the world. If there is no way to tell the difference between the real world and the experiences of a virtual reality, then it's possible we could be living in a virtual reality, but not know it.

Meditations on First Philosophy

René Descartes in his *Meditations on First Philosophy*, asks us to imagine an evil demon that has

> ...employed his whole energies in deceiving me; I shall consider that the heavens, the earth, colours, figures, sound and all other external things are nought but the illusions and dreams of which this genius has availed himself in order to lay traps for my credulity; I shall consider myself as having no hands, no eyes, no flesh, no blood, nor any senses, yet falsely believing myself to possess all these things.

This form of sceptical argument is very difficult to escape, and to this day haunts attempts to establish secure foundations of knowledge. Descartes' own solution was to invoke a benevolent God as a guarantee against the possibility that we're systematically deceived, but this is unconvincing.

A possible thought here is that though we cannot rule out the possibility that we are brains in vats, there is no evidence to support the contention. Normally, we don't take the mere logical possibility of something to be a good reason for countenancing its truth. So, for example, not many of us will take seriously the idea that a merry band of sentient garden gnomes lives in some remote part of the Amazon, just because it's a logical possibility.

However, the problem with this response is that we already know that if we're living in a virtual reality, then we won't have any evidence to this effect. In this situation, absence of evidence has no epistemological significance; in other words, we don't learn anything about the situation we're in by the fact that there is no evidence that we're inhabiting a virtual reality.

A World Within a World?

Perhaps the most promising approach to this puzzle is to attack the idea that our beliefs inside a virtual reality are necessarily false if they don't correspond to the world outside. For example, the philosopher Hilary Putnam has argued, roughl speaking, that the words that people use inside a virtual reality refer to the constituent elements of that world, rather than to anything that might exist outside the virtual reality. Therefore, whether or not I am currently typing this on a word processor depends on the state of affairs that exists in the particular world I occupy, whether this is a virtual reality or an embodied world of 'real' objects.

This line of argument suggests that Hugo need not worry too much about whether Orpheus is telling the truth. The real world just is the world he inhabits. Of course, if someone happens to turn off the computer that is generating his experiences, then he may end up reassessing what he thought he knew about the real world.

DID WE EVOLVE TO KNOW ABOUT THE WORLD?

(see pages 73-74)

The idea that there is a tension between the naturalistic origins of the human brain and the belief that our cognitive faculties are suited to the task of generating reliable knowledge is longstanding. For example, it is sometimes suggested that Darwin himself had doubts in this respect:

> ...with me the horrid doubt always arises whether the convictions of man's mind, which has been developed from the mind of the lower animals, are of any value or at all trustworthy. Would any one trust in the convictions of a monkey's mind, if there are any convictions in such a mind?'

Similarly, C. S. Lewis once claimed that '... the whole process of human thought, what we call Reason, is ... valueless if it is the result of irrational causes.'

Perhaps the first thing to say about all this is that there is plenty of evidence that shows that the brain does sometimes structure experience in a way that leads us into false belief. A good example of this sort of thing are the numerous visual illusions that have been identified by psychologists and others. However, as Michael Ruse has pointed out, the very fact that we're (often) able to identify when we're deceived by the brain, and also frequently able to explain this deception in evolutionary terms, suggests that our brains normally work fine.

Identifying Deceptions
Unfortunately, this response doesn't quite avoid the sceptical challenge. The problem is that in order to talk about being

able to 'identify' deceptions, and being able to offer 'evolutionary explanations' of them, it is necessary presuppose exactly what is being denied; namely, that the brain is able to generate accurate knowledge of the world.

If somebody is inclined towards the view that an organic entity, which evolved as a result of natural selection, is an unlikely source of knowledge about the world; and also that what we take to be true beliefs are actually convenient fictions that are useful in keeping us alive, but only if they seem warranted, then they're not going to be convinced that they're wrong by an appeal to theories and evidence that presuppose that the brain is a reliable mechanism for finding things out about the world.

The Ishmael Effect

Although it is hard to escape the sceptical implications of this sort of argument, there is something rather curious about it. Specifically, it seems to involve what philosopher David Stove has called the 'Ishmael effect', which refers to those occasions where philosophical arguments make exceptions of themselves. In this respect, it is significant that the argument outlined by the three bears relies on certain empirical claims – about evolution, genes, natural selection, and so on – which presuppose that there is a way to distinguish between true belief and false belief. In this instance, then, it is fair to say that the philosopher Simon Blackburn has a point when he states that 'the idea that there is something self-undermining about the relativist or sceptical tradition dies hard.'

QUICKIE SOLUTIONS

Chapter 1

1. He should choose the third room – lions that haven't eaten in three years will be dead.

2. They are three people: a grandmother, mother and granddaughter.

3. Yesterday, Today, Tomorrow.

4. c) VOLGE. If you rearrange the letters, you get HEAD is to HAT and HAND is to... That gives you GLOVE. VOLGE is an anagram of GLOVE.

Chapter 2

5. Alice is blind, and reading a braille book.

6. Your new salary is £268 per week. 4% of £250 is £10. You get an additional £8 on top of the 4% increase, so that's a total increase of £18. Therefore, your new salary is £250 + £18 = £268.

Chapter 3

7. Jack was a goldfish, Jill is the house cat.

8. 48 miles per hour. You can calculate this as follows. There are 225 minutes between 6.20pm and 10.05pm. If you divide 180 miles by 225 minutes, you find the average speed of the car in miles per minute (0.8 miles

per minute). If you multiply this by 60, you get the average speed in miles per hour – 0.8 x 60 = 48 miles per hour.

Chapter 4

9. The argument is invalid. Consider this equivalent argument: All insects are mortal. Women are mortal. Therefore, women are insects. Clearly that doesn't follow, because insects are not the only mortal things.

10. The straight lines are of identical length, though obviously it looks as if it's much longer in the bottom figure.

11. None of the people selected will have unlisted numbers. You selected the names from the phone directory.

12. She'll be 48 years old. Mary's brother is currently 8 years old (because 4 x 8 = 32). In 16 years time, Mary will be 48 and her brother will be 24.

Chapter 5

13. It's cheaper to take two friends to the theatre at the same time, because this way you only have to pay for your own ticket once.

14. They are on opposite sides of the river, so they are able to travel separately in the boat.

INDEX

A

afterlife, belief in 134–35
ambiguity effect 76–77
android puzzle 24–25, 93–94
Aronson, Elliot 49, 121–22,
     128, 130
Arthur, W. Brian 93
Asch, Solomon 49, 123
attractiveness 58–59, 125–126
     matching 62–63, 129–130
     f

B

Baggini, Julian 135
Barber Paradox 87–88
belief bias 90
beliefs, rational 64–65, 66–67,
     131–32, 133–34
Blackburn, Simon 139
Bowen, Charles 27
brain, cognitive ability of 72–73,
     138–39
brains in vats 70, 136–37
bystander effect 121

C

cannibalism 46–47, 113–15
Chrysippus 91
cognitive ability of brain 72–73,
     138–39
Crocodile Dilemma 22–23,
     91–92

D

Darwin, Charles 138
Descartes, René 112, 136
determinism 101, 30–31, 97–98
Dion, Karen 125
double effect, doctrine of 109–10
Downs, Chris 125

E

El Farol bar problem 94
Elevator Paradox 79–80
Ellsberg, Daniel 77
epidemic scenario 6–7
equal outcomes 77–78
eternal life 68–69, 133–34
Evans, Jonathan 90

F

Foot, Philippa 108
Frankfurt, Harry 97
Fuller, Lon L. 113

G

Gamow, George 79
Genovese, Kitty, murder of 121
group membership, effect of
     119–20

H

hallucinations 66–67, 131–32
Hempel, Carl Gustav 81
Hobbes, Thomas 52

hostility, inter-group 50–51,
    116–17
human nature 52, 119–20

I
inter-group hostility 50–51,
    116–18
Ishmael effect 139

K
Kahneman, Daniel 7

L
law arguments 113–15
logical equivalency 81
Lyons, Philip 125

M
Mackie, J.L. 111
Martian invasion 16–17
matching hypothesis 129–30
McGinn, Colin 73
mental worlds, existence of 95–96
mere addition paradox 85–86
metaphysics 27
Mignonette Case 115
Milgram, Stanley 49, 127, 128
monsters, belief in 66–67, 131–32
Monty Hall problem 39, 40–41,
    105–107
moral responsibility 30–31,
    97–98

Murstein, Bernard 129
mutuality factor 121–22

O
obeying orders 60, 127–28
omnipotence paradox 44, 111–12
other minds, problem of 28–29,
    95 96

P
paradoxical outcomes 91–92
Parfit, Derek 84–85, 86, 99
past attendance rule 93–94
personal identity problems 32,
    36–37, 99–100, 103–104
personality judgements 56–57,
    123–24
Piliavin, Irving 122
potential, question of 34–35,
    101–102
primacy effect 123–24
prisoner's dilemma 39
probability 10–11, 40–41, 76–78,
    105–107
Putnam, Hilary 137

Q
quantum indeterminacy 101–102

R
radical scepticism 65
Raven Paradox 14–15, 81–83

recency effect 123, 124
remote-victim experiment 127–28
Repugnant Conclusion 84–86
Robber's Cave experiment 50–51,
    116–18
Ruse, Michael 138
Russell, Bertrand 87

S
scepticism, radical 65
Sherif, Muzafer 49, 116, 117
snooker balls scenario 10–11
    solution 76–78
social psychology 49
Stern, Marvin 79
Stove, David 139

T
Tajfel, Henri 49, 119, 120
teletransportation 32, 99–100
Thomson, Judith Jarvis 108

torture 36–37, 103–104
Trolley Problem 39
    'loop back' variation 42–43,
    108-10
Tversky, Amos 7

V
valid/invalid syllogisms 20–21, 52,
    89–90
virtual reality 70, 136–37
Voltaire 27

W
Walker, John 92
Walster, Elaine 125
Williams, Bernard 103, 104

Z
Zeno's paradoxes 39
zombie 28–29, 95–96

PICTURE CREDITS
The publishers would like to thank the following for permission to reproduce images:
Cover images: iStockphoto
Alamy: p. 8, 38, 48, 64; Corbis: p. 26; Dreamstime: pp. 10, 21, 28, 32, 37, 42, 76, 82,
88, 89; Getty Images: p. 18; iStockphoto: pp. 3, 4, 15, 17, 18, 23, 24, 30, 33, 35, 37, 41,
45, 46, 47, 51, 53, 54, 58, 61, 62, 67, 68, 71, 72, 73, 74, 76, 83, 85, 92, 94, 95, 98,
100, 101, 103, 105, 108, 112, 115, 117, 120, 122, 124, 126, 130, 132, 134, 137.